IN PURSUIT OF DEGREES with INTEGRITY

A Value Added Approach to Undergraduate Assessment

prepared by
Northeast Missouri State University

published by
American Association of State Colleges and Universities

Copyright 1984 by American Association of State Colleges and
   Universities
      One Dupont Circle/Suite 700
      Washington, DC 20036-1193

Library of Congress Cataloging in Publications Data

In Pursuit of Degrees with Integrity

   Bibliography: p.
   Includes index.

   1. Northeast Misouri State University-Graduation requirements. 2. Northeast Missouri State University—Graduation examinations. 3. Norm-referenced tests—Missouri—Case studies. I. Northeast Missouri State University. II. American Association of State Colleges and Universities.
   LD4008.A54   1984   378.778'264   84-20519
   ISBN 0-88044-106-2

The opinions and recommendations in this book are those of the authors and are not intended to represent the official policy of the American Association of State Colleges and Universities.

Appreciation is extended to those who have helped build the Value-Added Program at Northeast: a talented faculty, an able administrative staff, and members of the Board of Regents—past and present—who supported us in this effort.

CONTENTS

Foreword .... Allan W. Ostar, President
American Association of
State Colleges and Universities

Preface .... Alexander Astin, President
Higher Education Research Institute,
University of California, Los Angeles

Prologue .... Charles J. McClain, President
Northeast Missouri State University

An Introductory Note

Chapter One .... A Case for Value Added

Chapter Two .... Planning for Value Added

Chapter Three .... Implementing Value Added

Chapter Four .... Value Added in Action

Chapter Five .... The Future of Value Added

Notes

Bibliography

Appendices

FOREWORD

The American Association of State Colleges and Universities is pleased to present this publication on the value-added program at Northeast Missouri State University. This program was awarded the 1983 G. Theodore Mitau Award for Innovation and Excellence in State Colleges and Universities, which is given each year to the institution that has demonstrated a strong commitment to academic improvement, innovation, and educational excellence. AASCU commends NMSU for its innovative approach to institutional program evaluation, as well as for making their experiences available to us through this case study.

Since the early days of the Academic Affairs Resource Center, AASCU has explored many methods of program evaluation that could enhance the integrity of the baccalaureate degree. We are certain that the value-added approach holds much potential for the future development and evaluation of institutional programs at state colleges and universities. Our AASCU institutions serve the public, and it is important for us to know whether we are fulfilling our institutional missions to provide high-quality educational experiences for the diversity of students we serve.

Allan W. Ostar
President
American Association of State
Colleges and Universities

PREFACE

While American higher education has long prided itself on its "diversity," the fact remains that most of the more than three thousand institutions that make up this vast system have come to embrace a remarkably narrow conception of "excellence." Basically, the pursuit of excellence, for most institutions, is equated with the mere pursuit of resources: money, facilities, highly trained faculty, and bright students. Those institutions that succeed in amassing a disproportionately large share of such resources are generally regarded as excellent, while most of the others tend to be regarded, at best, as mediocre.

The value-added approach to excellence represents a highly promising departure from this view. Rather than focusing on the mere acquisition of resources, the value-added view emphasizes how existing resources are used to enhance student learning. More important, the value-added approach does not take student learning for granted, but instead seeks to evaluate student learning and personal development through a sophisticated system of regular assessment procedures.

One especially attractive feature of the value-added approach is that it establishes a new set of institutional priorities whereby the learning and personal development of the individual student takes precedence over sheer competitiveness. Institutional attention is thus focused on how much each student is actually learning, rather than on normative comparisons regarding who is "best" and who is "worst." In addition, under the value-added approach, testing and retesting are carried out not so much for purposes of comparing students with each other, but more to provide feedback to students, faculty and administrators on the degree and extent of student learning. Decades of systematic research on human learning suggest that such feedback will significantly enhance the learning process.

What is particularly appealing about the Value-Added Program at Northeast Missouri State is that it has been implemented across-the-board. All participants in the academic community—faculty, students, administrators, and staff—are actively encouraged to devote their individual and collective efforts to this common task. And the implementation is not merely hortatory and theoretical. On the contrary, the commitment is backed up by an extensive computerized testing and data system that monitors each student's intellectual and personal development. Data are used not to threaten or punish, but rather to inform and enlighten as a basis for action. The case studies presented in Chapter Four suggest that this type of feedback can be used in a variety of institutional contexts to enhance student progress.

American higher education has a long history of resistance to innovation in its educational programs and practice. Classroom teaching, testing, and grading in most established institutions are carried out in very much the same manner today as was the case thirty or forty years ago. Except for a few new institutions that were consciously established to be "nontraditional," one is hard put these days to find institutions that have had the courage and foresight to adopt significant pedagogical innovations on an institution-wide basis. It is thus highly appropriate that the American Association of State Colleges and Universities chose to make Northeast Missouri State University a co-recipient of the 1983 G.

Theodore Mitau Award for Innovation and Change in Higher Education for this pioneering effort.

Alexander W. Astin
President
Higher Education Research Institute
University of California, Los Angeles

October 12, 1983

PROLOGUE

Through the years I became concerned that a student could accumulate 120 semester hours and yet be relatively untested intellectually. One solution to this problem is the use of external examinations. By requiring minimum scores on nationally normed tests for graduation, it is possible to insure that every student who receives a bachelor's degree will be knowledgeable in a discipline and in general education (liberal arts). Indeed, the use of external examinations provides a "safety net" for individual students, provides information about the quality of academic programs and the distributive requirements (liberal arts), and provides the ethos for planning documents.

Through the use of tests developed by some of the best minds in the disciplines, planning becomes much more intelligible. Agreement can be reached on what percent of graduates should be above the 50th percentile on a nationally normed examination, on the minimum score for graduation, and on how many students should graduate in each major. Once these goals are set, institutional decision-making about curriculum, resources, recruitment and other vital areas can be made on a more rational basis.

I hope that the story told in the pages of this book will be of value to other institutions of higher learning. Through the sharing of experiences, a new level of excellence in higher education can be reached.

Charles J. McClain
President
Northeast Missouri State University

AN INTRODUCTORY NOTE

"*If American higher education
is to forestall
the imposition of
a state system of examinations,
it will have to improve
its own forms
of quality control. . . .
If the academy
does not strengthen
these controls
of its own volition,
it may find
government moving to do so
in ways that jeopardize
the core of
the enterprise.*"

J. O'Neill[1]

AN INTRODUCTORY NOTE

Colleges and universities are beginning to feel the increased public scrutiny that has resulted from the dramatic report of the National Commission on Educational Excellence, "A Nation at Risk." While that report and its recommendations were targeted primarily to elementary and secondary education, one major impact on higher education has already been felt in the area of teacher training programs.

Over the last several years, state legislatures have been responding to public concern about quality in education by implementing statewide standards of competence for teachers. In its 1983 report on "The Condition of Teaching," the Carnegie Foundation for the Advancement of Teaching observed: "States are moving to institute tests for teacher certification at such a rapid rate that it is almost impossible to report the data before another state has decided to require a test as part of the certification requirements. These tests are taking several forms. Eight states are now testing the prospective teacher's basic skills as a prerequisite for entering the teacher education program . . . Many states are now also requiring teachers to achieve a passing score on a content area test. Georgia, for example, requires teachers to pass a criterion-referenced test in their teaching fields, e.g., English, biology, elementary education."[2]

There seems little doubt that colleges and universities will be called upon in the near future to take the next step: from comprehensive testing of the competence of prospective teachers to testing the achievement level of all bachelor's degree candidates. Several educational leaders are already urging this action:

" Operations by state as well as nongovernmental accrediting agencies to review the quality of educational programs and institutions require the measurement of both excellence and efficiency. Student growth of competence and level of competence at graduation, and efficient use of resources must all be assessed. Neither an institution that wastes its resources nor an institution that wastes the time and effort of its students, is an institution of quality."[3]

"But who should guarantee the competence of college students: the academy or the public at large?

Faculties of colleges and universities have traditionally established and maintained the standards for their own educational programs. In the coming years of public scrutiny, institutions wishing to retain control of the evaluation process will have to give greater attention to the relationship between student performance and institutional accountability.

As Clifford Adelman, commenting on the early work of the NIE Study Group on the Conditions of Excellence in Higher Education, told the American Council on Education board:

> "My sermon for you—and it is very much my sermon as an individual—is that before somebody less friendly... argues that the $180 billion investment we all make in higher education every year is not paying off, I think our college presidents ought to stop diverting our attention with the mythology that if only secondary schools were reconstituted in the image of higher education, if only we

jiggled our SAT cutoff scores for admission purposes, the 'crisis' in education would be all over."[4]

He urged that university leaders adopt a mode of protective anticipation, taking the "leadership in your own house before you find yourselves ... impelled to do so by external forces. The critical question is how institutions can go about this process of assuring themselves and the public that they are fulfilling their missions as institutions of higher education?"

The modern literature urges higher education institutions to adopt corporate models for evaluating and extending excellence, and to stay close to their primary missions. Thus, Naisbitt: "the question for the 1980's is 'What business are you really in?' " And Peters and Waterman: "Among the attributes of excellent companies is ... they 'stick to the knitting' ", i.e., " ... They stay reasonably close to businesses they know."

If the primary business of education is the advancement of learning, and if "the bottom line for assessing the effectiveness of any educational institution lies in the achievement and performance of students," then a value-added approach, locally adopted, will keep us focused on that business , help us do it better, and let us demonstrate that we do.

CHAPTER ONE

*"Value added"
means
that education
should make
a difference.
Value-added
assessment techniques
help institutions
show
that it does.*

A CASE FOR VALUE ADDED

In building a case for value added, this chapter focuses on the current crises confronting higher education, as well as traditional and the value-added responses to dealing with these problems. It also supplies some information on how value added relates to academic standards, measurements, and other data.

The Current Crises

Although the theme presented within the Introductory Note may be viewed as controversial in some circles, institutions of higher education do currently have a three-part mandate: 1) improve the quality of students' learning, 2) husband scarce resources, and 3) be accountable. A value-added model provides a unified response to these challenges.

Improving Student Learning

Colleges and universities are being called upon to help stem the "rising tide of mediocrity" in education.[5] Constituents of higher education are demanding evidence that demonstrates student achievement, command of subject matter, and mastery of basic educational objectives. They expect higher education to contribute to the solution of national problems. Several hypotheses seek to explain the current condition. Suggestions include: a loss of institutional focus during the rapid expansion of the sixties and seventies[6], overemphasis on research specialization[7], and a permissive social milieu[8]. But clearly higher education will not be afforded the luxury of scholarly reflection and debate before taking action on quality.

Husbanding Scarce Resources

In addition, institutions are being called upon to do more with less. In an era when optimists are those who describe the funding future as "uncertain," and when institutions can no longer look to enrollment growth to offset reductions in external funding, institutional advancement depends upon finding ways to make more effective use of existing resources. Many have turned to management models from the corporate sector, which emphasize "productivity", "efficiency", and "cost effectiveness". Coordinating boards, legislatures, and executive branches of state governments often use these concepts in evaluating and funding higher education. In response, to evaluate the effectiveness of education, local academic administrators study credit hours generated per faculty or department and determine cost per credit hour. Yet they do so with the tacit recognition that these parameters may have little to do with student learning or with the solution of national problems.

Becoming More Accountable

Given the limited dollars allocated to education, the trustees, the state, and the public demand evidence that their money is being used wisely and well.[9] Where institutions have been slow in responding to this demand, external agencies have seized the initiative through a state-mandated program review. But here, too, there is seldom provision for an accounting of the quality of education provided.[10]

The Traditional Response

Traditional approaches to institutional quality are generally based on "reputational" measures or "resource" measures.[11] Reputational measures represent the consensus of opinion of some expert group—typically deans, chairs, or senior scholars, and are the stuff of most "quality rankings." In fact, these measures are closely tied to an institution's admissions selectivity, its size, and the size and prestige of its graduate faculty. Resource measures, which include percentage of faculty with doctorates, number of faculty publications, expenditures per student, and number of library volumes, tend to be closely correlated with one another and with other measures of institutional "affluence." What evidence is available, however, indicates that neither reputational measures nor resource measures effectively predict the amount of learning that occurs at an institution.[12]

"Outcome" measures have become popular as alternatives to the reputation and resource approaches. Early versions of this approach focused on the proportion of graduates listed in Who's Who, the proportion admitted to graduate school, or the proportion who ultimately earn doctorates. More recent versions examine indicators such as the proportion of graduates who score above some level on a recognized "competency" exam (e.g., the National Teacher's Exam, or the Nursing Registry Boards).

The Value-Added Response

A value-added approach, which stresses student learning outcomes relative to student input potential, provides the means by which an institution can focus on educational quality. In making a commitment to quality, the institution also makes a commitment to using its resources to increase student learning in demonstrable ways. An institution can then be accountable for the learning it fosters as well as for the credit hours it produces.

As a concept, then, value added refers to the positive differences that an educational experience makes in a student's knowledge, attitudes, and skills. A value-added approach emphasizes the use of qualitative measurements to monitor student change and develops information which allows an institution to see how its actions influence that change. The basic argument underlying the value-added approach is:

> "that true quality resides in the institution's ability to affect its students favorably, to make a positive difference in their intellectual and personal development. The highest quality institutions, in this view, are those that have the greatest impact—add the most value—to the student's knowledge, personality, and career development."[13]

A Natural Setting

The value-added approach may be particularly useful for former "teachers' colleges" (and other institutions that have undergone relatively recent mission changes). As teachers' colleges, institutions could verify quality by their teacher placement record, by feedback from the principals and superintendents who hired their graduates, and by their close working relationships with the schools. As multipurpose institutions, these colleges and universities now produce graduates who must compete with graduates from the land-grant, large state, and private universities for graduate and professional school admission as well as for jobs. They are thus competing with students from institutions whose quality has been "assured" by their reputations, their resources, and their admissions standards. In the public's eye, those institutions possess quality; they entered the eighties with an image advantage.

In order for the former "teachers' college" institutions to meet the challenges of their new futures, they must substantiate their excellence. Yet many would find it difficult to do so using traditional quality measures. Though they boast strong faculties, these faculties, as a rule, do not emphasize research as much as teaching, and faculty research is a traditional measure of quality. Studies of the success rate of graduates, another traditional measure, may be premature for graduates outside the teaching fields. And certain reputational studies, or studies of admissions standards, may prove less than persuasive.

Rather, these institutions might do well to look to what they have long considered their strength: their effectiveness in teaching students. In a value-added approach, an institution gathers evidence to demonstrate that effectiveness.

At any institution, regardless of reputation or history, a focus on measures that evaluate outcomes relative to input potential reminds administrators, faculty, and students that the purpose of education is learning. A value-added institution, then, is one which asks 1) How well do we educate our students? and 2) What practices influence our ability to do so? Institutions interested in answering these questions assess changes in student performance and attitudes over time, and compare those changes to some desired outcome criterion.

Value Added in Operation

In operation, a value-added program works like this. A set of measurement devices is identified that are appropriate for evaluating a student's standing relative to some desired educational outcome. As Astin [14] notes, these measures might include standardized tests, performance samples, essays, departmental exams, interviews, and surveys. The last, surveys, are particularly useful where student attitudes weigh heavily in outcome goals.

Using these devices, initial measurements are made when a student begins a phase of the educational program (i.e., enters the institution, declares a major, or starts a course). These entering scores provide a profile of each student's strengths and weaknesses. As placement tools, these scores allow the institution to match curriculum alternatives to student needs. As counseling aids, these scores enable students to understand the rationale for that curriculum, and clarify the type and amount of improvement they must make. Most importantly, these initial scores provide a baseline for gauging subsequent performance.

As the students proceed through a course of study, the same or equivalent measures are again used to provide feedback on educational progress for students and the institution. Finally, when students complete that phase of their education, the same devices are again used as exit measures. By themselves, these exit measures may be used to certify terminal competency. When compared to each student's entry scores, they establish the "value added" by that educational experience.

Value Added and Academic Standards

Astin cautions that "A common misconception about the value-added approach is that it would somehow reduce academic standards."[15] The value-added approach does not recommend replacing 'A' for accomplishment with 'A' for improvement. Of itself, the value-added approach is neutral with regard to questions of what outcome levels of achievement should be expected of students. The standards issue is an important one, and many institutions may want to examine what absolute levels of performance they expect of their students, as well as what standards they set for content in the disciplines, for the preparation of teachers, and for the use of learning time.[16] But, while value-added measurements can be critically helpful in determining what students and institutions must do to reach some outcome goals, they do not tell institutions what those outcome goals should be. Rather, institutions remain free to determine what outcome proficiencies a degree should certify, or, as is the case of teacher education in several states, to have those proficiencies legislated.

Value Added and External Measurement

Most institutions would do well to include externally developed and normed measures as part of their value-added assessment program. Unlike using course grades and other local measures, using external measures demonstrates a school's willingness to meet a standard that it cannot unilaterally adjust. Course grades often tell little more than a student's relative standing in a class. Complementing these grades with external measures can indicate a student's progress in approaching that standard.

Perhaps more importantly, using test scores and other external measures of achievement helps separate the process of developing a student's competence from the process of certifying it. This, in turn, changes the relationship between the teacher and the student. If the assessments are external, the teacher becomes the student's collaborator in the effort to achieve a common objective, without also sitting as the student's sole judge.[17] External measures, then, help direct faculty attention to the rigor of their demands upon students, the adequacy of the curriculum, and the significance of grades as feedback.

Value Added and Other Data

An effective value-added program not only requires that students' performances be repeatedly measured, it also requires that the results of these measurements be linked with other information about students, and that composite profiles, at appropriate levels of aggregation, be accessible throughout the institution. Merging value-added achievement and attitude data with other management information (e.g., demographic, enrollment, financial aid, or housing data), allows institutions to determine what student characteristics and what institutional practices are related to value-added gains. (Most computerized student records systems can be adapted for this purpose.) The president, then, can have a clear profile of the total institution, while the schools and departments have a better understanding of themselves. Likewise, faculty members can have information about their individual students to help those students learn.

In theory, the value-added approach may be sound. In practice, moving to a value-added approach requires 1) careful preparation, 2) resolution of a number of implementation issues, and 3) the discerning use of value-added information to improve an institution's effectiveness. The following chapters discuss each of these steps.

CHAPTER TWO

*"Value added"
refers to
the positive influence
an institution has
on its students,
to the gains students make
toward desired goals.
An institution begins
by identifying
those outcome goals.
It then identifies
points in time
—from entry to completion—
when a student's progress
should be measured.*

PREPARING FOR VALUE ADDED

The process of operationalizing value added at a college or university is a demanding one. It requires 1) clear goals and objectives, 2) a relatively advanced capacity to collect data and monitor student progress, and 3) an evaluation strategy. This chapter concentrates on each of these prerequisites.

Goals and Objectives

Any assessment program is designed to further the goals of the institution. A value-added program enables an institution to demonstrate its effectiveness in developing students; it also helps an institution discover more effective ways to promote student change. But, the institution must begin with a clear understanding of which changes it wants to promote, and what goals it wants to set for its students. "Lacking an agreement on purpose, there cannot be clear criteria as to whether the outcomes ... are good in the ways intended."[18] That is, in order to determine the effectiveness of an institution, one must know "what it's about."[19]

Diversity of purpose is a fact and a strength of American higher education. It must also be a fact of assessment. Lawrence and Green note: "Different institutions and programs serve different constituencies and have different goals and objectives. To measure them all by the same yardstick is to do a disservice not only to the higher education system but also to prospective students and the public as a whole."[20] In a value-added assessment, an institution's effectiveness is judged by the progress its students make toward the goals it establishes.

The institutional mission statement may be a good starting place for establishing a consensus on an institution's goals for its students. These statements generally reflect the ways in which the institution defines its identity: its heritage, its values, its constituency, and its priorities. These statements are also, by their nature, broad and general; in some cases, they may be so broad as to be vague or ambiguous. What is needed, then, is to relate broad mission statement to more explicit, specific objectives, with particular emphasis paid to those that relate to student learning.

Many institutions will have already done this analysis, with the results stated as "Institutional Goals and Priorities," or "University Objectives." Departmental or school goals are often more specific still, with direct references to expected student outcomes. For institutions that have experience in "management by objectives" (e.g., Perlman) or "strategic planning" (e.g., Cope) this part of the exercise may be all too familiar.[21] Figure 1 illustrates a progression from mission statement to specific learning objectives using excerpts from Northeast Missouri State University publications.

Figure 1
From Mission Statement to Performance Objectives

Mission Statement (from draft report of the Commission II on Institutional Goals and Priorities 1985-1989)

"to achieve excellence through
1. a liberal arts based higher education,
2. nationally competitive pre-professional, professional and career oriented programs,
3. selected graduate programs at the master and specialist levels in areas that have achieved excellence at the undergraduate level,
4. pure and applied research efforts consistent with the teaching and public service functions of the university,
5. continuing education opportunities which meet national needs and are an outgrowth of existing programs,
6. public service"

Biology Program Objectives (from 1983-84 General Bulletin)

"to provide students with a broad background in biology"
"the logic and methodologies used in science as background for any career"
"an opportunity to specialize in one of several advanced areas in biology"
"qualify for admission to professional school...in medicine, dentistry"
"qualify a student for graduate school"

Performance Objectives-Biology (from Annual Program Improvement Report)

"to increase knowledge in general education (Science), as measured by the sophomore ACT exam, with an eight percentile increase in sophomore over freshman scores"
"to increase achievement in the major, as measured by the Senior GRE (Biology), with 57 percent of seniors scoring at or above the national average"
"to improve self reports of knowledge in the major field, as measured by the Graduating Student Questionnaire, by 5 percent over last year"
"to increase satisfaction with general education (Science), as measured by the Institutional Student Survey, by 5 percent"
"to increase satisfaction with quality of instruction in the major, as measured by the Institutional Student Survey, by 4 percent"

Data Collection and Monitoring Capability

In moving from learning objectives to a program for their assessment, it is essential that the institution have a model for the collection, storage, and analysis of information. A useful organizing scheme traces the student's relationship with the institution from initial pre-enrollment contact through graduation and beyond.

Such a scheme, which outlines the student's movement through the "university environment"[22] should also identify the student's principal points of contact with the institution at each stage. Thus, a prospective student may deal primarily with admissions personnel and may also communicate with the department in which he/she plans to major. Enrolled students interact extensively with the faculty. (At some institutions, underclassmen may deal mostly with the "general education faculty," while juniors and seniors may interact mostly with a partially distinct "departmental faculty.") But enrolled students also have frequent interaction with other segments of the institution. For example, campus residents may spend at least as much time with residence hall personnel as they do with faculty; all students have intermittent contact with the registrar's staff; athletes with the coaching staff; seniors may spend considerable time with the placement staff; and so on. Each of these points of contact is a potential source of influence on the student's development. Similarly, former students maintain some contact with the institution after graduation, most often through alumni and placement offices.

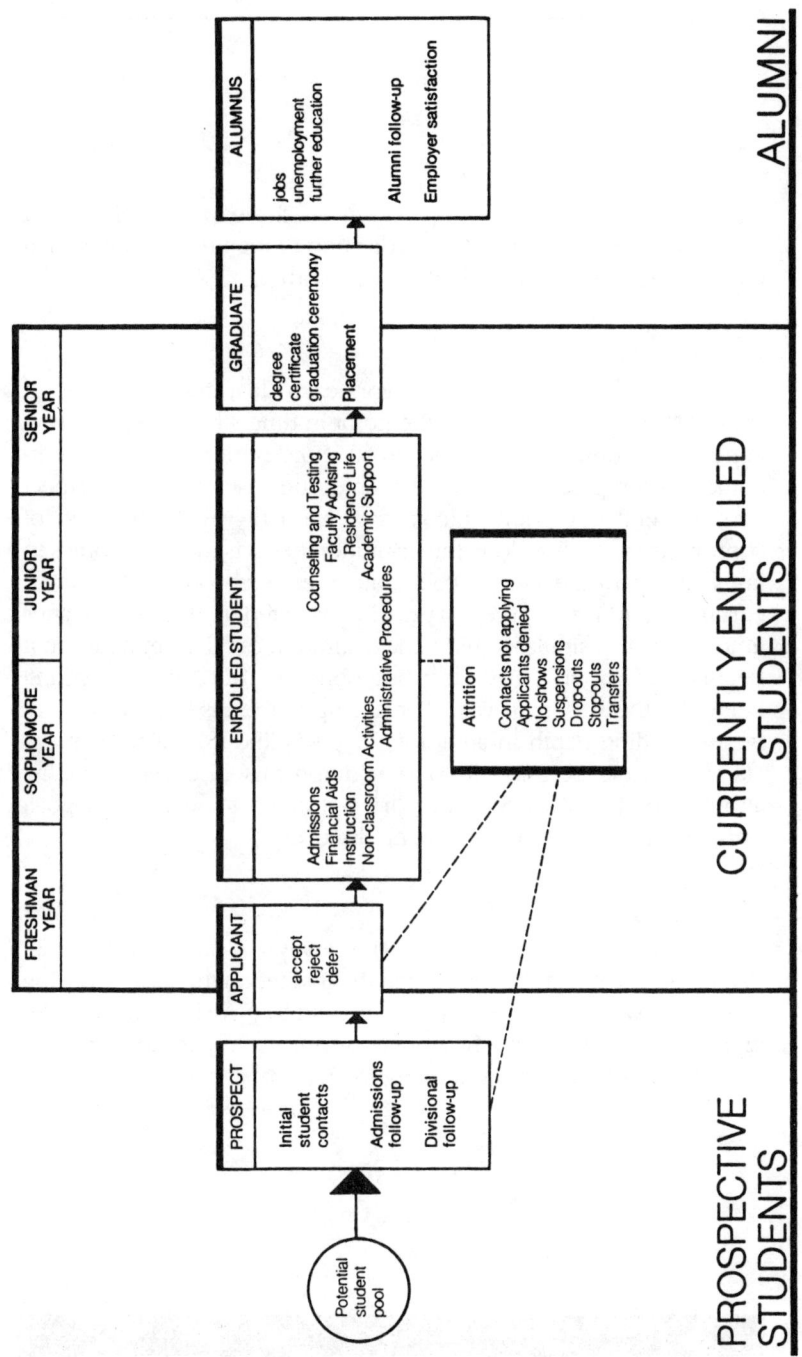

Figure 2

Each of these points of contact should be noted, along with an indication of the time span in which contact takes place. Figure 2 illustrates Northeast's scheme.

For each learning objective, it should be possible to identify the point in time when the institution expects that outcome to be achieved. Note here that not all "outcomes" await graduation. For example, the institution may expect most general education outcomes to be achieved by the end of sophomore year (how long the institution expects these outcomes to last is a separate matter). Other outcomes (e.g., job satisfaction or earning a graduate degree) may not be expected until sometime after graduation. In a similar fashion, the institution can determine when it begins working on a given learning objective. Here, not everything begins in the freshman year. For example, the institution may not begin building depth in an academic discipline until a student declares a major. Occasionally, an institution may discover ambiguity about when it really begins preparing students to attain some goal. This, itself, may be a very revealing discovery.

This analysis results in a model that identifies the time period when the institution thinks it is moving students toward each goal, and indicates the principal contacts between the institution and the student during each of these periods. A partial example is presented in Figure 3.

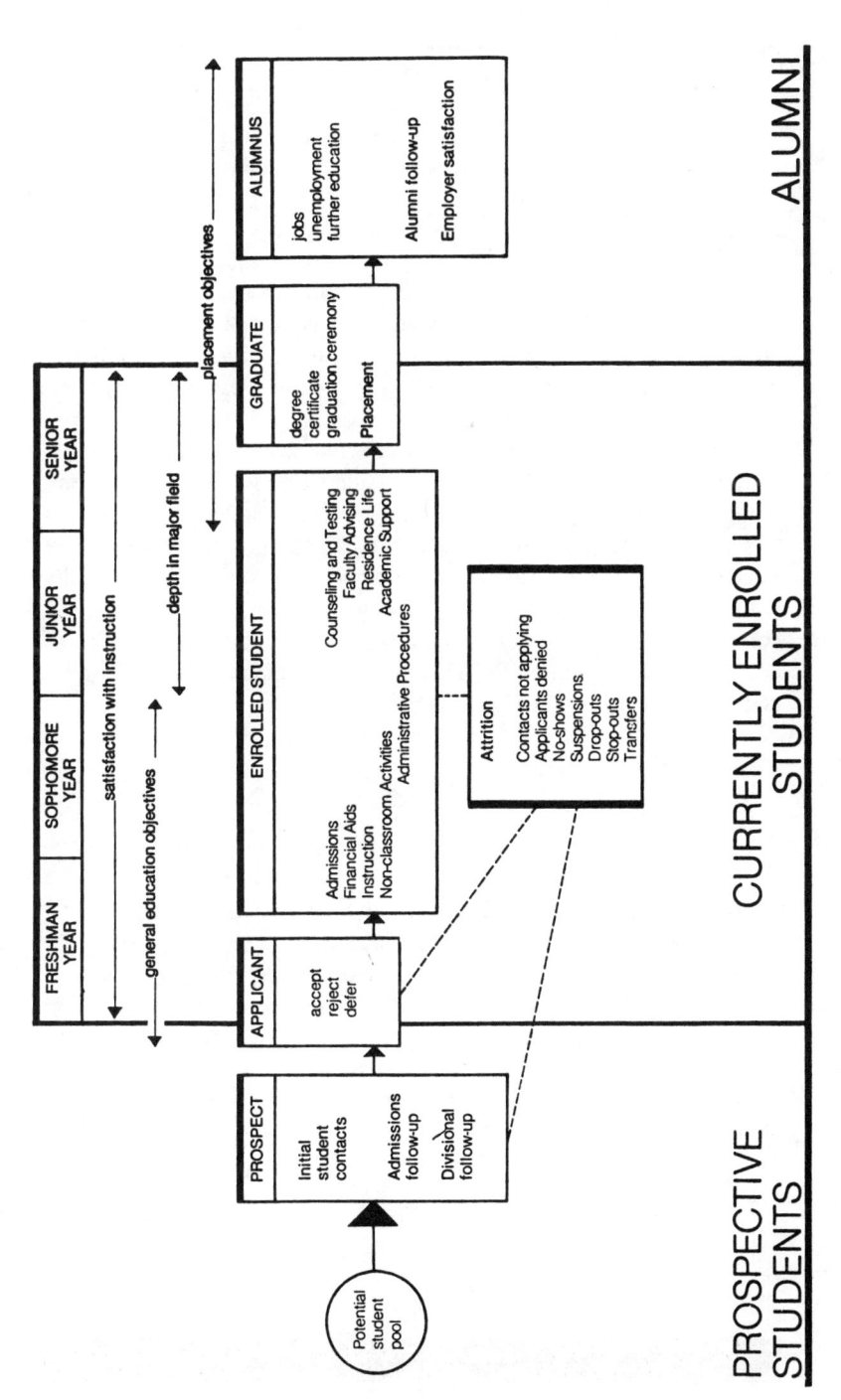

Figure 3

Evaluation

Examination of a model such as that in Figure 3 allows an institution to raise questions about its effectiveness. For example, how much depth of understanding in the major do students really gain from sophomore year to graduation? The model also enables an institution to ask questions about factors that may influence its value-added effectiveness. For example, most students are living in the residence halls while working on general education objectives. (At Northeast, most hall residents are freshmen and sophomores.) Could the residence hall staff contribute to student development in general education areas? Does it? Or, the faculty could influence the achievement of placement objectives. Do they? A complementary set of questions can be asked about each point of contact in the environment: What value-added gains does the Financial Aids Office affect? Counseling services? and so on.

To answer these kinds of questions, the institution needs to know how much a student develops from the beginning to the end of each phase; that is, it needs value-added measurements. The appropriate times for measurement have already been identified: "pretest" measures should be taken at or before the point in time when the institution first begins working on an objective. "Posttest" measures should be taken at the point when the institution expects the student to have attained that objective. In the case of objectives that span a considerable length of time (e.g., attitudes toward instruction over four years), midpoint measures may also be desirable.

Evaluative Instruments

The selection of measurement devices remains. The range of options (standardized tests, surveys, etc.) was mentioned above, as were some of the advantages of using externally developed instruments. In addition, an institution would do well to avoid reinventing the wheel. A wide range of instruments, covering a broad variety of learning objectives, are available from Educational Testing Services (ETS), American College Test (ACT), National Center for Higher Education Management Systems (NCHEMS), and other agencies. An institution should review these instruments before setting out to devise an instrument of its own. A list of instruments used at Northeast Missouri State University appears in Appendix A. In some cases, since quality is multidimensional, an institution may choose to use several measures (e.g., a test and a survey) of progress on the same objectives.

An institution planning to implement a value-added program should also consider building on whatever measures may already be in place. For example, most freshmen arrive with either ACT or Scholastic Aptitude Test (SAT) scores, even when those scores are not required for admission. Their scores are on file (somewhere) on campus. Residual testing of those students who arrive without scores, followed by retesting of all students with an alternate form of the same test a year or two later, may provide a satisfactory measure of the value added in English and math (along with natural science and social science if the ACT is used). Similarly, seniors bound for graduate school probably already take the Graduate Record Exam in their discipline, the Medical College Admissions Test, or other national admissions tests. Institutional copies of score reports are routinely returned (somewhere) to the campus. Since these are probably a select group of seniors, these data alone would provide a positively biased measure of exit competency in those areas. An institution might consider having all seniors in appropriate disciplines take these exams. Administration of a form of the exam to sophomores or juniors as a pretest is also useful. Finally, some student surveys may already be in place. Using and expanding on these data might be preferable to initiating a parallel program.

Other Important Data

In addition to measurements specifically taken for value-added purposes, the institution should review other data already available at the times when students begin and end each phase of a program. For example, most student records systems would already track a student's grade point average, residence status, hours earned, and financial aid status as they are when that student takes a posttest in general education. This information combined with a student's pretest scores may prove quite helpful in determining what factors influence general education gains. Figure 4 summarizes the value-added and demographic data maintained on students at Northeast Missouri State University.

In Sum

Several considerations, then, guide preparation for value added. The institution must specify its expectations for student learning, decide when its milestones are to be reached, and select appropriate measures. Figure 5 is a planning checklist that was helpful at Northeast.

Preparing to implement a value-added program, such as the program itself, is a dynamic process. Upon beginning a program, an institution will discover new questions about itself and its students. What begins as a simple effort, with a few measurement devices, may in time evolve into a fairly complex system. At Northeast, several measurements were added well after the program began; others are now being considered. A few false starts occurred as well. As the measurement process was refined, a number of issues—some related to measurement, some not—proved to be crucial to the success of the program. The following chapter outlines those issues.

STUDENT DATA RECORD

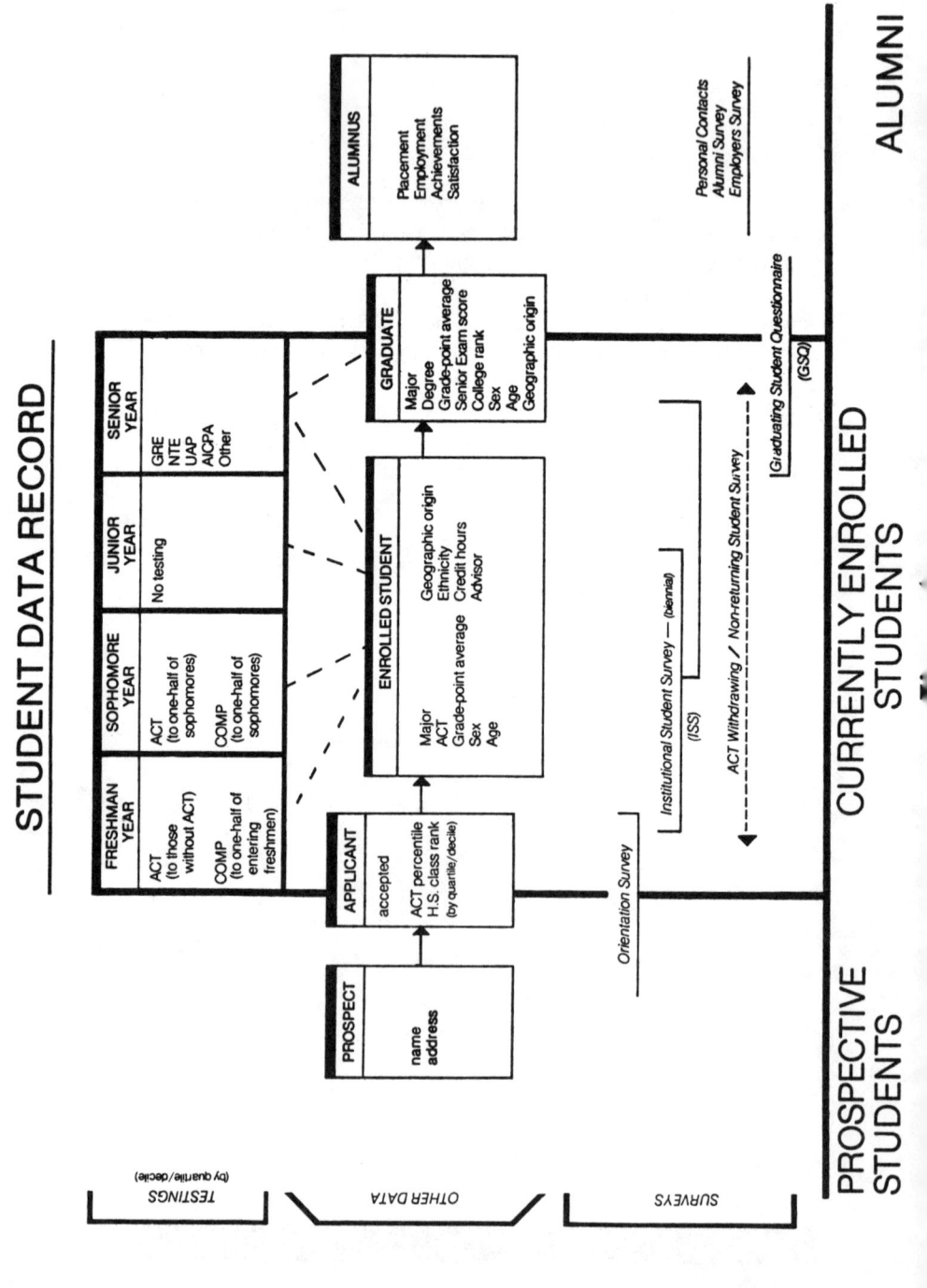

PROSPECT
name
address

APPLICANT
accepted
ACT percentile
H.S. class rank
(by quartile/decile)

FRESHMAN YEAR
- ACT (to those without ACT)
- COMP (to one-half of entering freshmen)

SOPHOMORE YEAR
- ACT (to one-half of sophomores)
- COMP (to one-half of sophomores)

JUNIOR YEAR
No testing

SENIOR YEAR
- GRE
- NTE
- UAP
- AICPA
- Other

ENROLLED STUDENT
Major
ACT
Grade-point average
Sex
Age
Geographic origin
Ethnicity
Credit hours
Advisor

GRADUATE
Major
Degree
Grade-point average
Senior Exam score
College rank
Sex
Age
Geographic origin

ALUMNUS
Placement
Employment
Achievements
Satisfaction

Orientation Survey

Institutional Student Survey — (biennial) (ISS)

ACT Withdrawing / Non-returning Student Survey

Graduating Student Questionnaire (GSQ)

Personal Contacts
Alumni Survey
Employers Survey

TESTINGS (by quartile/decile)

OTHER DATA

SURVEYS

PROSPECTIVE STUDENTS | CURRENTLY ENROLLED STUDENTS | ALUMNI

27

Figure 5

Preparing for Value Added—A Checklist

1. Do key individuals agree on the institutional mission? on learning objectives for students?

2. Is there a model which follows a student from prospect to alumnus? Does the model identify points of contact along the way?

3. When does the institution begin working on each learning objective? When does it expect a student to have accomplished each objective?

4. Are aptitude data available for students entering each phase? Can missing data be obtained?

5. Are outcome data on comparable measures available for students completing each phase? Can missing data be obtained?

6. Do measurement devices permit comparisons with external standards or norms?

7. Are pre- and post-measures available for each learning goal?

8. Are attitudinal goals included along with cognitive goals? Is progress measured?

9. What demographic and academic information is available for each student? Is it linked to value-added data? Is it maintained on the same computer?

10. Have potential relationships between support services and student improvement been identified? Are there measures to examine those relationships?

11. Is there computer capability to examine information at the individual student level? at the departmental level? at the institutional level?

CHAPTER THREE

"The Commission and its staff
found it odd
that large-scale research
on growth and change
in college students
has focused
on every conceivable topic
other than
their academic learning...
If measures of educational
progress
come to
a screeching halt
when people reach the age
of seventeen,
we give
the false impression that
education and learning
stop
at this age as well."[23]

IMPLEMENTING VALUE ADDED

As an institution contemplates implementing a value-added approach what are some of the concerns it will have to face? This chapter considers various issues regarding 1) the basic challenges (e.g. time, fears of data abuse, comparisons), 2) assessing quality, 3) measurement and curriculum, 4) student motivation, and 5) validity.

The Basic Challenge

Several educators have speculated about the reluctance of institutions to implement a value-added program. Astin makes the observation that the value-added approach is a "time-consuming, expensive, and potentially divisive method of assessing quality."[24] The costs in time and money are real, and cannot be ignored; but they are not overwhelming. The concern about divisiveness may be. A successful value-added program requires broad support throughout the campus. Such support is built on open communication and trust.

An extensive value-added program cannot be implemented overnight. Successful change is a gradual process; Northeast began in 1973. A readiness for improvement and a respect for the responsible use of data develop gradually.

Controlling Blame and Taking Credit

Faculty, administrators, and staff must remain mindful that the goal of a value-added approach is to increase student learning. Inevitably, some data will be disappointing. Rather than pointing fingers, everyone should be encouraged to examine how their contributions could produce more positive change. More often, the data will demonstrate remarkable growth. But, just as pinpointing blame is harmful, so too is seizing credit. All must believe their efforts have made a difference.

Maintaining Open Communications

Value added improves student learning because it provides knowledge of results. In view of this, institutions would do well to remember that administrators and faculty are learners too. As implementation proceeds, channels for informal, verbal, and personal communication provide feedback on the implementation process itself. Attending to and acting on that feedback improves the process and keeps it on track.

Dealing with Fear of Data Abuse

When a segment of the institution first becomes involved in a value-added program, its members quickly realize the potential for negative uses of information. Some may fear that data are really being collected to allow "someone at a higher level" to address a private agenda (e.g. close a program, cut a budget, deny a promotion). Several steps may help alleviate these concerns.

Foremost is not to use value-added performance data to support negative decisions. Saying "no" is an unpleasant task, familiar to administrators and faculty alike. Procedures for supporting such decisions were established before value-added data were available. Those procedures should not change rapidly. Just as opportunities for abuse are soon realized, so too restraint is soon respected. Strategies to improve weaknesses are often different from strategies to eliminate them.

Analyzing Versus Interpreting Data

Data should be used early in setting goals and seeking ways to improve. Here, prior analysis of data is helpful; prior interpretation is not. There should be broad participation in interpreting the data to identify strengths and weaknesses. When individuals help interpret data, they are more likely to support acting on it.

For example, for several years Northeast students have earned ACT-English scores when tested at the end of sophomore year that are substantially higher than the scores those same students had earned at or before admission. Interpretation by the faculty attributed much of this gain to a required competency-based freshman English course. Closer examination of the data also indicated that students who entered with high scores were not showing subsequent gains. Once some of those students were involved in the discussion, it was discovered that many had substituted Advanced Placement or CLEP credit in English for the freshman course, and had neither been required nor encouraged to take further writing courses. Both students and faculty supported changing that procedure. Hasty interpretation of this data might have led to the false conclusion that faculty were teaching below the level of their best students.

When value-added data have been used to establish goals, they should also be used to review goal attainment. Good measures will show evidence of achievement. Faculty, staff, and students will support a process that demonstrates the results of their efforts.

In addition, broad support exists for including quality factors in academic planning. While there will and should be discussion about the appropriateness of any particular measurement device, most academics will prefer plans based on learning to plans based on credit hour production.

Making Comparisons

When reviewing data at the program level, historical comparisons (e.g, How do this year's senior business majors compare to last year's?) are helpful in establishing trends and detecting the results of program changes. In contrast, cross-sectional comparisons (e.g, Why do business majors gain more than English majors?) are divisive. They may also be misleading since the two programs may use different measurement tools. Where comparisons are sought, using the total institution as the reference group (Why do business majors gain less than the institutional average) is generally less controversial. The important point is that, in value-added terms, one unit's (i.e., one student's or one program's) gains need not be achieved at the expense of another unit's losses.

Measuring Quality

As interest in a value-added program spreads through an institution, a number of recurring issues will be raised. Some of these may focus on the idea of "measuring quality." One position is that the quality of an education is intangible and by its nature cannot be assessed. Astin dubs this the "nihilist view," and observes that it ignores judgments about the quality of undergraduate colleges and programs that are made every day.[25] Students make them when deciding which college to attend, faculty make them when deciding where to apply for a position, and so on. The real issue, then, is on which basis these judgments are to be made: reputation, resources, or evidence of learning.

The case for judgments made on value-added measurements should not be overstated, however. Even the best single measurement tool offers only an approximation; multiple indicators may improve this approximation, but it is unlikely that even the broadest battery of instruments would capture the full richness of the learning experience. Enthoven commented on this in 1970:

> "This experience taught me that one should not expect to find an all embracing criterion of value added or effectiveness, and such criteria usually aren't necessary for improved allocation decisions. Simply, crude indices can be very useful. This and similar experiences inspired a motto: It is better to be roughly right, than exactly wrong."[26]

Mixing Cognitive, Affective, Psychomotor Elements

Related concerns address the relative emphasis on cognitive versus non-cognitive (i.e., attitude, value, or satisfaction) measurements. Some may object that cognitive measures are, by themselves, cold or sterile. Since this same question of relative emphasis can be raised about the institutional mission, it is vital that the mix reflected in the measurement package be consistent with the mix reflected in the institutional mission. A broad range of instruments that assess student attitudes, values, and beliefs are available.[27] Locally developed supplements also may help assess emphases unique to the institution.

Evaluating Life Long Effects

Others may insist that the only true measures of quality are the success and satisfaction of graduates throughout life. As a practical matter, few institutions can wait that long to obtain feedback on their effectiveness. But long-lasting influences are important. Some measurement devices do attempt to gain evidence about these effects. ACT's College Outcome Measures Program (COMP) may be of interest here.[28] COMP uses a variety of instruments to assess changes in six areas of lifelong learning: 1) Communicating 2) Solving Problems 3) Clarifying Values 4) Functioning within Social Institutions 5) Using Science and Technology, and 6) Using the Arts. Northeast currently samples students with COMP instruments at three points: at entry, at the end of the sophomore year, and at the end of the senior year. Plans are also being made to sample alumni with COMP instruments at various stages after graduation. Humanities faculty have been particularly interested in the "Problems," "Values," and "Arts" indicators, since these areas are not included in the traditional ACT test.

Surveying Alumni

Alumni measures, of whatever type, also assist in addressing questions about long lasting and/or delayed effects. Northeast's experience has been that alumni are generally more receptive to surveys than to "tests." In selecting or designing alumni instruments, particular care should be taken to insure that measurements obtained from a segment of alumni can be directly and unequivocally compared to measurements obtained from that same cohort while they were students.

Measurement and Curriculum

"Teaching to the Tests"

A separate set of issues concerns the relationship between measures and the curriculum. A prominent issue is that of "teaching to the tests." Actually, two different issues are often discussed under this rubric. The first, a content issue, questions whether the content of a particular measurement device adequately represents the content of that portion of the curriculum it claims to assess. The second, a score validity issue, questions whether students will be "coached" for a test.

The content question can only be answered after both the curriculum and the measurement instrument have been carefully reviewed. Faculty will generally be more familiar with the former. Initial questions about test content are often based on partial information gained from the publisher's descriptive material, a glance at sample items, or second-hand reports from students. Nothing can substitute for careful review of the actual instrument.

If standardized tests are used, a word of caution is in order. Examination copies can be obtained if appropriate provisions are made for test security. But, by design, standardized tests attempt to make fine distinctions across the full range of achievement, including the upper extreme. As a consequence, they contain what may seem like an unusually large number of difficult items. Very, very few test takers are expected to answer these items correctly. Said differently, the proportion of items which may be missed while still obtaining a "good" score is much higher than one would usually find on a classroom test. Individuals reviewing standardized tests need to understand this clearly, or they will overestimate test difficulty.

At Northeast, a few faculty have chosen to go an extra step, and actually take the examination used in their discipline. Arrangements were made to destroy institutional copies of score reports unopened, so that only the faculty member received the results. In four known cases, the faculty members were later quite willing to disclose that they had scored at the 99th percentile on the tests taken [the GRE in three different disciplines, and the National Teachers Exam (NTE) in Social Studies]. These faculty members no longer question the appropriateness of test content.

Reviewing Curriculum

Review of test content may also stimulate productive curriculum review. For example, when faculty in a discipline find a topic emphasized on a national test that is not emphasized in their curriculum, they may be motivated to rethink their position on the importance of that topic. Clearly this area affords room for healthy disagreement among scholars. In some cases, de-emphasis or omission of a topic may be deliberate; in others, it may have been through oversight, or because "No one's picked that up since Professor Smith retired." In yet other cases, the curriculum that is stated in the catalog may not be the curriculum that students actually follow ("We haven't offered that course in several years.") Once faculty are familiar with the content of a test, value-added performance data on the test help faculty make curriculum decisions based on what students are actually learning.

Deciding on Test-Taking Strategies or Techniques

The validity issue questions whether student scores might be artificially raised through last-minute or short-term test preparation or coaching. This controversial issue is not limited to value-added programs; Messick and Jungeblut[29] review the research literature with regard to coaching for the SAT. Several observations seem noteworthy. First, several nonspecific test taking strategies (e.g., read the instructions in advance, do not linger over difficult items) may contribute to test performance. Many students will have long since been familiar with these; however, since these strategies probably also contribute to performance on classroom tests, an institution might consider reviewing them with entering students. Second, preparation in the content area of the exam will improve scores. Third, and most importantly, the amount of score improvement is in proportion to the time and effort spent in preparation. Thus, short-term (i.e., six to twelve hours) preparation produces gains which, though real, are so small as to be generally inconsequential. More extensive preparation (semester or year long) produces larger gains, but here the distinction between "coaching" and "schooling" blurs. The conclusion, then, is that when students learn, test scores improve. This conclusion is not inconsistent with value added.

Responding to Unavailable Tests

Another curriculum-related issue concerns those learning objectives and components of the course of study for which no appropriate assessment devices are available. For example, Northeast has been unable to locate externally developed instruments appropriate for assessing progress toward program objectives in Agriculture and certain areas of Home Economics. Here, an institution should consider developing its own measurement devices. Some of the shortcomings of local instruments have already been discussed. In addition to the investment of time and resources required to develop an instrument properly, the institution will not have the ability to compare the performance of its students on that instrument to that of similar students elsewhere. Over a period of years, however, data from local instruments can be useful in demonstrating trends and in determining the effectiveness of program changes. In any case, a local measure is preferable to no measure at all. In addition, using a local measure in those areas avoids the potentially deleterious effects of exempting students in selected areas from the assessment process. Sometimes an institution may find a middle ground by using an external measure for some objectives of a program and supplementing it with additional, locally developed items.

Value Added and Grading

A final curriculum issue is the relationship between value-added assessments and grades. Given the diversity of grading practices generally in use (including criterion-referenced grades, norm-referenced grades, mastery approaches, and a family of seemingly unrelated techniques collectively called "grading on the curve"), it is seldom clear how one should expect students' value-added performance changes to be related to their grades. The issue is further clouded when some composite measure of grades (e.g., cumulative GPA) is used. Moreover, a discussion about value added and grades is fraught with all the complexities and sensitivities associated with any grading discussion.

Nonetheless, the issue will be raised, most often when value-added assessment differs substantially from grade assessment. At the outset, one should insure that the value-added measurements and the grades under discussion attempt to assess performance on the same objectives. For this purpose, four-year cumulative GPAs are seldom helpful; recomputation of the GPA for relevent courses may be. It is also helpful to remember that both value-added measures and grades attempt to indicate something about what a student has learned. Maintaining a focus on student learning is quite valuable in untangling grading discussions. In fact, where the goal emphasizes learning the most, rather than earning the highest grade or the highest score, grading discussions tend to resolve themselves.

At Northeast, reversal of a ten-year grade inflation trend has been a welcome, if not fully anticipated, consequence of the value-added program. There has been no institutional dictum about grading. Yet faculty concerns, occasioned by value-added measurements, about topics such as whether they were expecting enough from their students, whether essential points of content were adequately covered, and whether comprehensive examinations should be given at the end of each course have been followed by both increases in value-added gains and decreases in the proportion of A's assigned. The change has not been precipitous.

Rather, most students report they "can still earn the same grade; it just takes more work".

Student Motivation

Other validity issues consider whether some particular score or set of scores can be trusted; whether they really measure what they purport to measure. These are similar to the coaching issue discussed above.

Whether students were motivated to do their best on a particular test is one such question. This need not be a worry for baseline ACTs or SATs taken prior to college admissions, for students know that important decisions may be influenced by these scores. It is relevant to tests taken while enrolled. Several options are available. The most powerful, although not the most expedient, is to persuade students that the tests are important, both to evidence their own accomplishments and to improve the institution. Pride and the need for achievement are powerful motivators. When students believe that assessment is legitimate and important, their motivation can be almost overwhelming. (Some Northeast students now raise complaints such as, "How can I prepare for my sophomore test when my history teacher is out sick so often?")

Faculty Attitudes

Since student attitudes often reflect faculty attitudes, the faculty must be persuaded first. This is somewhat hampered by the perennial anecdote about the student who marked choice "C" for every item and left the exam after five minutes. Having faculty proctor the examinations discourages this, and also helps to dispel the myth that it happens with great frequency. Appropriate comparative data are also helpful in responding to this concern (e.g., "Why should this year's students be less motivated than last year's?")

Voluntary Versus Compulsory Approaches

Of course, student motivation can be insured by making important student rewards (e.g., graduation, entry into sophomore year, grades, or scholarship renewal) contingent on demonstrating some specific value-added gain. Minimum competency requirements are now in place or being discussed in a variety of areas; these generally require some output measure without regard for input potential. While such requirements may be ultimately desirable, a prudent institution would want evidence that it is effective in developing some competency before it required all students to demonstrate it. A similar caveat applies to the frequent suggestion that students be motivated by posting all test scores to their transcripts. Here, too, an institution would probably want to develop an understanding of how its grades relate to its test scores before posting both measures to the same permanent, and widely disseminated, document.

When the value-added measurement program was first instituted at Northeast, all testing was optional but strongly encouraged. The dean sent personalized letters to each student to be tested, explaining the nature and purposes of the test, and the ways in which the data could assist the student and the university. Testing was scheduled at a time and day convenient for students. A make-up schedule was established for students who were unable to attend the first administration. The campus media were also enlisted in reminding students about the test dates. The initial compliance rate was quite high, and improved each subsequent year. After five years of such voluntary testing, the Faculty Senate passed a resolution requiring the testing of all students. In fact, this resolution was designed to affect the, by then, very small number who were not participating in the voluntary program. An indication of the current level of student support for the program can be gained from the excerpts from student-edited publications which appear in Appendix B.

The "Poor Test Taker"

Another validity issue stems from the observation that "Some people just don't test well." In some cases, this observation refers to the phenomenon of test anxiety, which does handicap the performance of a number of students. Considerable information as to the causes, extent, and remediation of this problem is available (e.g., Anderson and Helmick).[30] Since this phenomenon also affects classroom testing, an institution might determine if it provides appropriate support services. In other cases, the observation reminds institutions of the need for suitable testing conditions for special needs students. In yet other cases, the observation refers to the assertion that students knew more than they were able to remember that day. If the institution makes arrangements for retesting of students who were ill or otherwise distracted while taking a test, this should not remain a major concern.

Other Validity Issues

Survey Research Data

Validity questions are also raised about survey data. Generally, these ask whether self-reported information is accurate. Here, too, extensive literature on the extent and nature of bias to be expected is available (e.g., Owens).[31] In most cases, it appears that distortions are not serious. This question is most frequently raised when a survey result is surprising or counterintuitive. In this instance, it may be helpful to interview a sample of the group surveyed. Additional confidence may also be gained when different groups (e.g., freshmen, seniors, and alumni) report the same condition. Finally, it is often reasonable to assume that whatever bias is present is roughly constant, and so is corrected for (i.e., subtracted out) in value-added comparisons.

When conducting surveys, institutions will need to make a decision about anonymity. Anonymous surveys may be more credible, and may also yield a higher return rate. However, they preclude a value-added analysis at the individual respondent level. Alternatively, including a request for name and/or student identification number, along with an appropriate disclaimer about the use and disclosure of data, may be preferred. As a compromise, an anonymous survey that does request relatively detailed demographic and academic information (e.g., major, year of graduation, GPA) may be sufficient for making before/after comparisons on small groups without identifying individuals. Northeast uses this approach on many of its surveys.

Variation in Student Input Characteristics

Two issues may be raised about the validity of value-added changes. The first concerns changes in student input characteristics. In a laboratory environment, student input characteristics would be kept unchanged while the effect of program manipulations on student outcomes was assessed. On campuses, this is seldom possible or desirable. As a result, some will question whether changes in institutional quality simply reflect changes in the input characteristics of the student body. ("Of course you're doing better; you're getting a better prepared freshman class.") If outcome measures of quality alone are being used, this is a valid criticism. But comparing outcome achievement to input potential is exactly the point of value added. Thus, true gains in effectiveness would be those in evidence after adjusting for input changes. A clear understanding of this dimension of value added provides an appropriate response to this question.

The Regression Effect

A final validity issue refers to the "regression effect" which occurs whenever repeated measures are used. In simplest terms, by chance alone, scores above the mean are likely to decline, scores below the mean are likely to improve. This discussion rapidly becomes technical, and will probably be of most interest to measurement specialists. The evaluation research literature (e.g., Struening and Guttentag)[32] contains extensive discussions of this statistical artifact and various techniques to adjust for it. However, the current opinion seems to be "Acknowledge the problem, and go on."

Once an institution has initiated a value-added assessment program, it has significant opportunities to use the information from that program to improve its effectiveness. The following chapter describes and illustrates several of those opportunities.

CHAPTER FOUR

*Value-added measurements
help decision makers
focus
on the effectiveness
of the educational process.
From this perspective,
the major challenge is
to search for
patterns and characteristics
that make
a difference
in learning.*

VALUE ADDED IN ACTION

Sound decisions require judgment and facts. When an institution knows the facts about its impact on student learning, it is in a position to evaluate alternative courses of action in terms of their potential influence on how much students learn. Decisions based on quality are sometimes remark ably different from decisons based on credit hour production. Sometimes, too, improvements are made at the expense of some cherished old myths. This chapter offers five case studies designed to demonstrate how the value-added approach has provided the perspective and mechanisms for solving concrete problems. The cases include 1) sophomore tests: A case study for improving general education, 2) senior tests: eliminating the "soft track," 3) survey data: improving student satisfaction, 4) academic growth in the fraternity system, and 5) increases and improvements: value added and the budget process.

Natural starting places for attempts to increase student learning are the classroom and the curriculum. An example from Northeast's Division of Business illustrates how the availability of data reflecting changes from freshman to sophomore year helped identify and resolve a problem in mathematics.

Sophomore tests: A Case Study for Improving General Education.

Prior to and during 1979, sophomore test results for all business majors indicated an increase, over entering performance, in all skill areas of the ACT with the exception of mathematics. The results of Northeast business graduates taking the GMAT also revealed a weakness in the mathematics area.

The data gained from the sophomore tests and the GMAT prompted concern among the business faculty. The lack of mathematical skills could affect the performance of business majors in various upper-division business courses. The lack of the same skills among the seniors probably caused lowered scores on the graduate school admissions tests as well as possible difficulties for students seeking jobs.

Curriculum committees within the various business disciplines—accounting, business administration, and business education—discussed several alternatives for improving the mathematical skills of business students. The mathematics faculty was also consulted during the deliberations.

In May of 1979, the curriculum committee recommended a stronger math course be required of all four-year business majors in the general education curriculum requirements. The University approved the recommendation and it became effective during the 1979-80 academic year. Subsequent to the strengthened mathematics requirements, sophomore test scores in that area were significantly increased. Since then, though the entering ACT scores for business majors have also increased, sophomore tests reveal further gains in mathematics.

Changing a course requirement is a straightforward response to an easily understood problem. In the prior example, it was also an effective response. In fact, adding a course is often the reflexive response to any and all academic problems. But sometimes the cause of a problem is more subtle. In the following example, when facts challenged a myth, the first response was to attack the facts and defend the myth.

Senior Tests: Eliminating the "Soft Track."

Between 1970 and 1975, the number of students majoring in psychology tripled. As the University added new faculty, the range of courses offered in the program increased; and the number of specific courses required of all majors was reduced to permit students to sample widely from this range. The program boasted a strong reputation, based primarily on faculty credentials and enrollment.

Performance of seniors on the Psychology GRE, however, challenged this reputation. During the first five years of testing, only 34 of 109 students tested scored at or above the national average and in 1976, only one of fourteen graduates scored above the 50th percentile.

Faculty response to this information proved typical of faculty reactions in programs with disappointing value-added data. The initial response was to question the appropriateness of the testing instrument. Perhaps the content of the GRE was too advanced or too specialized. However, once the faculty reviewed the exam, they concluded that it focused on material adequately covered in the curriculum.

Attention then turned to student test-taking motivation. Since the program required no minimum score for graduation and posted no scores on student transcripts, students might not be taking the test seriously. Occasionally, anecdotes about students who approached the test in a frivolous manner lent some credence to this possibility. Yet, it was not apparent why psychology students should be less motivated than students in other campus programs who consistently performed at a higher level. Moreover, faculty efforts to increase student test-taking motivation (for example, by telling advisees that their performance would influence letters of recommendation) showed no impact on subsequent GRE scores.

Administrators and faculty then analyzed the relationship between GRE scores and other academic measures. Entering ability, as indicated by ACT scores and high school class rank, was found to be comparatively typical of the general student body and only weakly related to GRE performance. Neither overall grade point average nor grade point average in psychology courses predicted senior test performance. But, detailed analysis of transcripts divulged a pattern of course selection that related to GRE scores. Many students with low GRE scores and average or better grades took a large number of enrichment courses (e.g., Psychology and Mass Media), skill course s (e.g., Biofeedback Practicum) and independent readings courses. These same students tended to systematically avoid elective courses in traditional core areas (e.g., developmental, learning, social). Finally, student grades in the former set of courses proved consistently higher than in the latter. In short, many students followed a "soft track" through the curriculum.

The faculty unanimously adopted a curriculum revision for entering students, reducing electives and requiring a more balanced sequence of courses for all students. Through advising, these same standards were implemented for students already enrolled under the former curriculum. At the same time, the program made efforts to bring grading criteria in enrichment and experiential courses into line with those in other courses.

Two classes have graduated since these changes were made. Each class performed at the national average (Figure 6) and major course grades now predict GRE performance. And, to the surprise of some faculty, student satisfaction with the program as reflected on the Graduating Student Questionnaire improved during this period as well.

The Psychology senior test example demonstrates the use of several interrelated measures (senior GRE, entering aptitude, overall GPA, GPA in the major, and enrollment information) in decision making. It is also a case in which an action aimed at an achievement measure influenced a satisfaction indicator as well. In other cases, survey data about student satisfaction may be what stimulates a change. A case study from Northeast's Nursing Division illustrates this use of survey data.

Figure 6

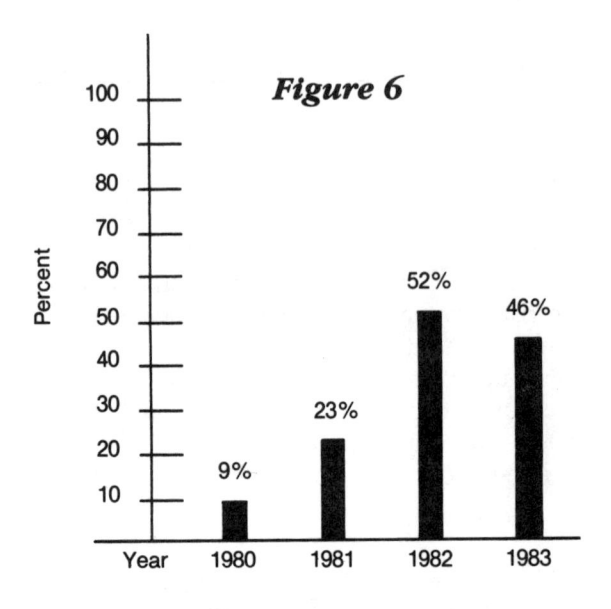

Percent of Psychology Majors Scoring above 50%-ile On GRE-Psychology Senior Examination

Year	1980	1981	1982	1983
Percent	9%	23%	52%	46%

Selected Items of the Graduating Student Questionnaire: Responses of Graduating Psychology Majors (Undergraduate only)

Item	\multicolumn{5}{c}{Weighted Means}
	1980	1981	1982	1983	1984
Increase Knowledge	2.53	2.57	2.63	2.70	
Major Courses	3.53	3.21	3.41	3.35	
General Ed Courses	2.76	2.97	2.95	3.13	
Quality of Instruction	3.24	3.14	3.15	3.30	
Faculty Advisement	3.00	2.71	2.91	2.95	
Library Services	2.76	3.17	3.31	3.35	
Availability of Courses	2.76	3.28	3.07	3.48	

Survey Data: Improving student satisfaction

Although the Graduating Student Questionnaire (GSQ) is not the only measure of student attitudes and perceptions of the University environment, the survey does provide a composite picture of the University's effect on students completing a program. The GSQ, from nursing students, provides the nursing faculty with data concerning their graduates' perceptions of the value added to their nursing ability by general education courses, nursing major courses and University services and activities. Graduates' opinions about the nursing program are vital to the nursing division in attracting quality applicants and in maintaining positive relationships with community agencies where clinical laboratories exist for students, and where graduates seek employment.

As the halo effect from the 1978 accreditation of the program by the National League for Nursing began to wear thin, scores on the GSQ hit an all-time low in 1980. The nursing faculty and the division head set out to reverse the negative attitudes toward Northeast and the nursing program. The program instituted a one-credit professional socialization course as an elective, taught by the division head, to provide a forum where students could broaden their horizons regarding current issues in nursing and their imminent transition into the working world. The course proved so valuable that it has now become a requirement for senior nursing students.

The program also encouraged students to participate more on nursing faculty committees and in decision making involving student learning needs and experiences. The faculty encouraged more unity within the nursing student body; students elected class presidents and representatives to faculty committees.

The faculty increased contact with advisees and students in lower division courses by providing an early fall picnic, better academic advisement, more faculty participation in applicant interviews, more contact with prospective students and their families who visit campus, and a panel discussion and information session where upper division students provide information to freshmen, sophomores and prospective students about junior- and senior-level nursing courses.

The results of these efforts became apparent with the 1981 graduating class. The 1981 GSQ showed improved student satisfaction with the nursing program and with the overall university. This finding was replicated by the 1982 and 1983 graduating classes. Moreover, student satisfaction may have contributed to increased learning as well. The Nursing Division uses the State Nursing Board exam, which is not taken until several weeks after graduation, as their senior exam. In 1981, 1982, and 1983, 100 percent of the graduates passed their exam on the first attempt.

In the Nursing example, several initiatives were made simultaneously. As a result, although the total package was effective in producing the desired changes in satisfaction, the data do not permit assessment of the individual effectiveness of any one of the changes. This is poor experimental science, but is perhaps typical of action oriented research. The Nursing faculty is now conducting a follow-up study, using some locally devised supplementary instruments, to determine more precisely which variables contribute to satisfaction in Nursing.

Faculty, then, find value-added measurements helpful in addressing traditional faculty concerns: whether the students are gaining in their ability to read, write, and do mathematics; whether they are developing an appropriate depth of understanding in their major fields; whether they are positive in their attitudes toward learning and satisfied with their educational progress. At least as important, however, are the opportunities for other members of the university community to demonstrate their contribution to achieving educational goals. For example, Northeast's fraternities were reminded that they were academic, as well as social, organizations.

Unexpected Spin-off: Academic Growth in the Fraternity System

The Northeast Missouri State University social fraternity system (13 national organizations) achieved a long-term goal during the spring 1983 semester. For the first time since beginning computation of fraternal academic reports in 1978, the overall fraternity grade point average (GPA) matched the "all-men's" undergraduate GPA of 2.50. This is in contrast to the 1978 fraternity academic report which noted a .24 difference—a 2.62 all-men's GPA versus a 2.38 fraternity GPA.

The emphasis on academic growth within the fraternity system developed out of a number of specific and subtle changes within the system in promoting higher standards. In the spring of 1978, the system initiated chapter reports to illustrate the productivity of pledge programs. In the fall of that year, the system put out a comprehensive "Fraternity Academic Report" which included active-member GPAs. Through this report, it became obvious that the fraternity system lagged well behind the all-men's undergraduate GPA. This discovery led administrators, faculty advisers and chapter presidents to initiate discussions to develop common strategies for higher standards.

These discussions were followed by a two-year period of academic growth. During the fall of 1980, the difference between the all-fraternity and all-men's GPAs narrowed nearly 80 percent. To achieve this, the fraternity system initiated such actions as reactivation of annual awards for academic programs. The Interfraternity Council (IFC) also passed a bylaw in 1979 prohibiting any student with less than a 2.00 GPA from pledging a social fraternity. More subtly, they released chapter academic records to campus media as incentives.

With incentives to increase GPAs, chapter members examined their study habits and classroom performance. The University commitment to a value-added education for each student prompted faculty to develop higher performance expectations. Despite positive efforts of chapter members, the rate of fraternal academic growth, based on GPAs, declined. The margin of difference between the all-men's GPA and the fraternal GPA widened by 31 percent from the previous semester.

This trend resulted in a renewed challenge to the system to improve academic performance among its members. Early in January of 1982, an IFC task force submitted a proposal to the Dean of Students, suggesting that scholarships be provided for fraternities that excelled academically and that punitive action be taken against fraternities that did not meet minimum GPA standards for two consecutive semesters. Parity with the all-men's GPA was to be reached within two years of the policy approval.

The IFC formally accepted the IFC Academic Standards Policy in March of 1982. The GPA goal was reached within that academic year. That result was particularly encouraging since the fraternity system met its projected goal one year ahead of time. Though excited and pleased with these results, the IFC and Northeast's fraternities realize continued evaluation of the policy's effectiveness is necessary.

Each of the preceding examples illustrates decisions which resulted in increasing the institution's effectiveness through the improved use of existing resources. Having cost virtually nothing, these improvements are necessarily cost effective. However, some goals do have dollars attached. The hiring of additional faculty, the development of current faculty, the purchase and replacement of equipment, and the improvement of facilities may all be directly related to the achievement of academic goals. Value-added measurements allow an institution to demonstrate a relationship between expenditures and achievement. Northeast currently bases internal and external budget requests for noninflationary increases on value-added performance measures.

Increases and Improvements: Value added and the budget process

Prior to 1979, the state of Missouri's appropriations for higher education for general operations were based almost exclusively on enrollment-driven formulas. In 1979, Missouri's Coordinating Board for Higher Education asked institutions to suggest items for additional funding that were specifically designed to improve the quality of their educational programs. Northeast responded to this opportunity by submitting a request that included value-added performance improvements.

Since 1974 Northeast had been assessing performance at the individual student, discipline, and divisional level. For external purposes, however, it seemed desirable to use a set of global performance measures that preserved the integrity of the measurement concept while focusing only on the central dimensions of institutional achievement. The measures chosen were institution-wide gains on the nationally normed sophomore and senior tests and institutional averages on the graduating student questionnaire. Since these instruments had been used for several years, they lent themselves to historical comparisons. Year to year performance gains with and without supplementary improvement funding could also be assessed. With continued funding, longer term gains (e.g., the performance of the 1980 freshman class on the 1984 senior exams) could also be evaluated.

This value-added performance based approach was received favorably by the state. Despite submission at a financially difficult time for Missouri, 48 percent of the requested value-added funds, or $407,868, was appropriated for targeted improvements in language and literature, science, mathematics, and business.

Subsequent years' improvement requests were submitted in this format and accompanied by a report of the measured performance changes during the previous fiscal year. After reviewing the 1981 request, the Governor prepared a budget recommendation which stated:

"Northeast proposes to document substantial increases in measures of institutional quality in return for this funding. The Governor highly commends the institution's bold initiative in developing and applying such measures and recommends that all other institutions follow Northeast's example."

Figure 7 is an extract from Northeast's 1985 request. Currently, Northeast leads the state in program improvement appropriations per FTE student.

In preparing the fiscal year 1985 budget recommendations, Missouri's Commissioner of Higher Education stated: "The staff is recommending specific program improvements at two institutions. These recommendations address research needs that are unique to the University of Missouri, and an instructional project of national acclaim at Northest Missouri State University."

Instructional Budget Summary

General Knowledge

INSTITUTIONAL PERFORMANCE GOAL, BUDGET FY 1985:

NMSU aims to increase the knowledge and understanding in general education as measured on the sophomore American College Testing Residual Exam (ACT) and the College Outcome Measures Project (COMP) with a four percentile-point increase in sophomore scores over freshman scores; to increase student ratings as indicated on the Graduating Student Questionnaire (GSQ) in (1) overall satisfaction toward general education by .05, and (2) cultural awareness and participation in cultural and social events by .06; to increase student ratings to 2.70 in the following as indicated on the Institutional Student Survey (ISS): (1) instruction in writing, (2) understanding and applying mathematics, (3) understanding different philosophies and cultures, (4) understanding and applying scientific principles, (5) understanding the interaction of man and his environment; and to raise satisfaction with computer services indicated on the ISS by .14.

Personal Service	1985 Program Improvements		Quality Performance Measurements	1983	1984	1985	w/Imprv.
$120,165	Five FTE Faculty		SOPHOMORE TEST:				
			ACT%-ile increase	2.0	2.0	2.0	4.0
			COMP%ile increase	2.0	2.0	2.0	4.0
Equipment and Operations	1985 Program Improvements		GSQ:				
$41,020	$ 2,000	Faculty Development	Overall rating of General Education	2.91	2.91	2.91	2.96
	9,000	Program Review	Cultural awareness	2.14	2.14	2.14	2.20
	17,000	New Personnel Costs	ISS:				
	9,000	Computer Software	Instruction in writing	2.66	2.66	2.66	2.70
	3,520	Professional Services	Understanding/applying math	2.46	2.46	2.46	2.70
			Understanding cultures	2.54	2.54	2.54	2.70
			Understanding/applying scientific principles	2.46	2.46	2.46	2.70
$161,185			Understanding interaction of man and environment	2.64	2.64	2.64	2.70
			Computer services	3.01	3.01	3.01	3.15

The addition of five FTE faculty in the area of General Education will allow the institution to place more emphasis on personalized learning as a result of reduced class size and teacher load. More individualized assistance and interest can be given to the students by the faculty. Faculty morale and preparation time will be improved. This personal concern will increase student motivation toward learning and increase satisfaction toward the general education curriculum; this in turn will affect positively knowledge gained through the comprehensive, interdisciplinary learning experiences within the general education requirement.

The monies requested for the computer-assisted instruction and other software will increase the students' awareness and knowledge of computer and other skills which are a growing requirement in good job placement for graduates. The professional services of consultants and guest clinicians will stimulate, reinforce, and enrich both faculty and students.

When preparing internal budget recommendations for program improvements the various divisions select their objectives based on their analysis of prior value-added data and request the funding allocations they deem appropriate for achieving these objectives. Figure 8 is an example from Northeast's Division of Language and Literature.

As can be seen, the improvement objectives are specific and the level of attainment with and without improvement funding is projected. In this fashion, then, decisions about personnel, operations, and equipment funding, both external and internal, are tied to their demonstrable impact on student learning.

The favorable response of public policy makers in Missouri may be indicative of a national trend. The following chapter discusses this possibility and its implications for the conduct of higher education.

Language and Literature Division

PERFORMANCE GOAL - BUDGET FISCAL YEAR 1985: To improve the quality of instruction and services to effect gains in achievement within the academic major as indicated on the senior examinations with 67 percent scoring above the 50th percentile of the national norms; to increase the Graduating Student Questionnaire (GSQ) averages (1) by .03 on the improvement of courses in the major, and (2) by .03 in assistance in career planning; to effect an increase in the ratings on the Institutional Student Survey (ISS) relative to the following: (1) writing effectively by .05, (2) speaking effectively by .05, (3) course content in the major by .03, (4) instruction in the major by .03, and (5) out-of-class availability of instructors by .04.

	Personal Service	
	1985 Program Improvements	
$48,066	Two FTE Faculty	
	Equipment and Operations	
	1985 Program Improvements	
$ 2,000	Faculty Enrichment/Development	
2,000	Program Review	
7,000	New Personnel Costs	
	Total	
	1985 Program Improvements	
$59,066		

	Measurements			
Variable	1983	1984	1985	w/imprv.
No. of Majors	390	400	410	
Degrees	84	90	81	
Credit Hours	13,226	13,564	13,900	
SENIOR EXAM:				
% achieve 50%-ile	64%	64%	64%	67%
GSQ:				
Improve courses in major	3.21	3.21	3.21	3.24
Assist with career plans	3.04	3.04	3.04	3.07
ISS:				
Instruction in writing	3.05	3.05	3.05	3.10
Instruction in speaking	2.85	2.85	2.85	2.90
Course content in major	2.97	2.97	2.97	3.00
Instruction in major	2.92	2.92	2.92	2.95
Out-of-class availability	3.16	3.16	3.16	3.20

Rationale Narrative

With the increased number of students, additional faculty will effect some reduction in class size and greater availability of instructors. This increase in personnel and the operations funding will serve to maintain current standards of excellence and achieve some small gain. The provision of computer software materials for use by students, the development of writing tests, the increase in student/faculty ratio will impact the student achievement and attitudes. Implementing a writing proficiency for all divisional majors, improving instructional resources, employing two additional faculty, and providing faculty development opportunities will make possible improved instruction and achievement and be reflected in improved examination scores and student satisfaction.

CHAPTER FIVE

*The favorable response
of policymakers
in Missouri
to the value-added approach at
Northeast Missouri State
University
represents a positive step
in assuring the public
of the quality
of its higher education
programs.*

THE FUTURE OF VALUE ADDED

Other institutions may not implement the value-added approach in precisely the same fashion; in fact, they ought not to, since focusing on the institution's mission will, of necessity, lead each college down its own highly individual path of quality enhancement.

Nevertheless, these elements of NMSU experience stand out as watchwords for other institutions:

"NMSU began with the conviction that it wanted to know how much it was actually contributing to student learning. NMSU built upon the assumption that student growth is influenced by the entire institution, and therefore involved the university at all levels in the assessment program.

NMSU realized that gaining the knowledge about each student's growth results from extensive and repeated assessments by a variety of means, hence the reliance not simply on standardized tests but on attitudinal data, student questionnaires, and financial and housing data as well.

NMSU understood that faculty involvement is the key to a successful value-added effort. NMSU obtained this involvement through eleven years of proving to faculty that they would be supported for being honest about evaluations.

NMSU helped each academic division to identify and set specific performance goals, which could utilize ability, achievement, and attitudinal data.

NMSU identified areas needing program improvement in order to more effectively and efficiently contribute to the mission of the institution.

NMSU learned that the student performance data collected in value-added assessments was helpful in substantiating requests for budgetary increases tied to program needs."

As a model or an approach, value added has not yet reached its full potential, particularly with respect to implementation. So, what direction should its development take? What are some of the "next steps" needed to make this concept even more viable?

With respect to monitoring student progress within the lower level cognitive domain of educational development, NMSU has made notable inroads in finding useful instruments for measurement. Yet, a need continues for valid, reliable indicators of the more advanced cognitive levels as well as the affective and psychomotor domains. NMSU has available revised questionnaires that demonstrate the potential to meet some of the need for the affective domain, thereby monitoring changes in the attitudes, values, and resulting roles of the individual student. However, the search for indicators in the psychomotor domain is generally just beginning. The sooner institutions are able to incorporate a broader list of measures of student growth, the sooner they will be able to convince critics that value added is much more than the simple comparison of student growth against curriculum objectives.

One of the truly exciting potential uses of the value-added approach concentrates on planning. As institutions learn more about themselves at a descriptive level, they will begin to explore explanations as to why progress is or is not occurring. Although it would be currently presumptuous to claim a predictive capability for value added in the near future, the descriptive/explanatory inroad will allow for systematic planning at the university-wide, division, discipline, and (of particular interest) the individual student levels.

In addition to plotting actual progress of students in the various domains of education, advisors should attempt to develop "expectation models" for their students. In other words, based on established levels of academic ability and motivation, the advisor would be able to project and ultimately compare a student's gains with the "expected" gains for students with comparable academic and motivational levels within the national sample. If this were accomplished, then the institution could approach a true assessment of the value added to the student's development through its programs.

NOTES

[1] J. O'Neill, "Examinations and Quality Control" In *Meeting the New Demand for Standards,* ed. J.R. Warren (San Francisco: Jossey-Bass, 1983), pp. 69-80.

[2] C. Feistritzer, *The Condition of Teaching: A State by State Analysis,* (Princeton, N.J.: The Carnegie Foundation for the Advancement of Teaching, 1983).

[3] J. Stevens and B. Hamlett, "State Concerns for Learning: Quality and State Policy" In *Meeting the New Demand for Standards,* ed. J.R. Warren (San Francisco: Jossey-Bass, 1983), pp. 29-38.

[4] C. Adelman, quoted in "Campuses Urged to Take the Lead" In *Higher Education and National Affairs,* Vol. 33, No. 4 (March 9, 1984).

[5] National Commission on Excellence in Education, "A Nation at Risk: The Imperative for Educational Reform" (Washington, D.C.: U.S. Department of Education, 1983).

[6] A. Christ-Janer, "Institutional Mission in an Era of Retrenchment" In *Liberal Education,* Vol. 66 (1980), pp. 161-168.

[7] G.W. Bonham, "The Mission of Higher Education in Contemporary Society" In *Liberal Education,* Vol. 66 (1980), pp. 121-131.

[8] *The Rise and Fall of National Test Scores,* ed. G. Austin and H. Garber (New York: Academic Press, 1982).

[9] F. Kiehle, "The Use of State Level Goals as the Basis for Assessing Postsecondary Education Performance" In *ERIC ED 211 024* (Governor's Committee on Postsecondary Education, October 1981); L. Marcus, A. Leone and E. Goldberg, "The Path to Excellence: Quality Assurance in Higher Education" In *AAHE-ERIC* (Washington, D.C., 1983).

[10]R.A. Scott, "Program Review's Missing Member: A Consideration of Quality and Its Assessment" In *ERIC ED 167 015* (1980).

[11]A. Astin, "Why Not Try Some New Ways of Measuring Quality?" In *Educational Record* (Spring 1982), pp. 10-15.

[12]H. Bowen, *The Costs of Higher Education* (San Francisco: Jossey-Bass, 1980); A. Astin, "Undergraduate Achievement and Institutional 'Excellence'" In *Science,* Vol. 161 (August 16, 1968), pp. 661-667.

[13]A. Astin, "Measuring the Quality of Undergraduate Education" In *Proc. of Conference on Quality of Baccalaureate Education* (Austin: University System of Texas, 1981).

[14]A. Astin, "A National Study of Minorities: Some Implications for Undergraduate Education" In *Forum for Liberal Education,* Vol. 5, No. 3 (1983).

[15]Astin, "Why Not Try Some New Ways of Measuring Quality?", pp. 10-15.

[16]C. Adelman, "Getting Up Off of the Floor: Standards and Realities in Higher Education" In *AGB Reports* (July 1983), pp. 13-19.

[17]A.C. Enthoven, "Measures of the Outputs of Higher Education: Some Practical Suggestions for Their Development and Use" In *Outputs of Higher Education* (Washington, D.C.: WICHE-ACE/CRDHE, July 1970), pp. 51-58.

[18]M. Keeton, "An Approach to a Theory of Quality Control" In *Report on a Conference on Quality Control in Nontraditional Higher Education* (Columbia, MD: Antioch College, 1974).

[19]R.M. Hutchins, "Interview with Robert Maynard Hutchins" In *Chronicle of Higher Education* (May 23, 1977).

[20]J.K. Lawrence and K.C. Green, "A Question of Quality: The Higher Education Ratings Game" In *AAHE-ERIC/Higher Education Research Report No. 5* (Washington, D.C.: AAHE-ERIC, 1980).

[21]P.Perlman, "New Tools and Techniques in University Administration" In *Educational Record,* Vol. 55 (1979), pp. 34-42.; R.A. Cope, "Strategic Planning, Management, and Decision-Making" In *AAHE-ERIC Higher Education Research Report No. 9* (Washington, D.C.: American Association for Higher Education, 1981).

[22]A. Astin and R.J. Panos, "The Education and Vocational Development of College Students" *The American Council on Education* (Washington, D.C., 1969).

[23]C. Adelman, "The Major Seventh: Standards as a Leading Tone in Higer Education" In *Meeting the New Demand for Quality,* ed. J.R. Warren (San Francisco: Jossey-Bass, 1983), pp. 39-55

[24]Astin, "Why Not Try Some New Ways of Measuring Quality?", pp. 10-15.

[25]Astin, "Why Not Try Some New Ways of Measuring Quality?", pp. 10-15.

[26]Enthoven, "Measures of the Outputs of Higher Education: Some Practical Suggestions for Their Development and Use", pp. 51-58.

[27]K.A. Feldman and T.A. Newcomb, *The Impact of College on Students* (San Francisco: Jossey-Bass, 1969).; A. Astin, "Four Critical Years: Effects of College on Beliefs, Attitudes and Knowledge" In *ERIC ED 149 657* (1977).; H. Bowen, *Investment in Learning* (San Francisco: Jossey-Bass, 1977).

[28]A. Forrest, *Increasing Student Competence and Persistence: The Best Case for General Education* (Iowa City, IA: American College Testing, 1982).

[29] S. Messick and A. Jungeblut, "Time and Method in Coaching for the SAT" In *Psychological Bulletin,* Vol. 89 (1981), pp. 191-216.

[30] S.B. Anderson and J.S. Helmick, *On Educational Testing* (San Francisco: Jossey-Bass, 1983).

[31] W.A. Owens, "Background Data" In *Handbook of Industrial and Organizational Psychology* (Providence, RI: Brown, 1970).

[32] *Handbook of Evaluation Research,* ed. E. Struening and M. Guttentag (Beverly Hills, CA: Sage, 1975).

BIBLIOGRAPHY

Adelman, C. "Getting Up Off of the Floor: Standards and Realities in Higher Education." *AGB Reports,* July 1983, pp. 13-19.

----------. "The Major Seventh: Standards as a Leading Tone in Higher Education." In *Meeting the New Demand for Quality.* Ed. J. Warren. San Francisco: Jossey-Bass, 1983, pp. 39-55.

----------. quoted in "Campuses Urged to Take the Lead." *Higher Education and National Affairs,* 33, No.4, March 9, 1984.

Anderson, S.B., and J.S. Helmick. *On Educational Testing.* San Francisco: Jossey-Bass, 1983.

Astin, A. "A National Study of Minorities: Some Implications for Undergraduate Education." *Forum for Liberal Education,* 5, No.3, 1983.

----------. "Four Critical Years: Effects of College on Beliefs, Attitudes and Knowledge," 1977 (ERIC ED 149 657).

----------. "Measuring the Quality of Undergraduate Education." *Proc. of Conference on Quality of Baccalaureate Education.* Austin: University System of Texas, 1981.

----------. "Undergraduate Achievement and Institutional 'Excellence.'" *Science,* 161 (August 16, 1968), pp. 661-667.

----------. "Why Not Try Some New Ways of Measuring Quality?" *Educational Record,* Spring 1982, pp. 10-15.

Astin, A., and R.J. Panos. "The Education and Vocational Development of College Students." *The American Council on Education.* Washington, D.C., 1969.

Austin, G., and H. Garber, eds. *The Rise and Fall of National Test Scores.* New York: Academic Press, 1982.

Bonham, G.W. "The Mission of Higher Education in Contemporary Society." *Liberal Education,* 66 (1980), pp. 121-131.

Bowen, H. *The Costs of Higher Education.* San Francisco: Jossey-Bass, 1980.

----------. *Investment in Learning.* San Francisco: Jossey-Bass, 1977.

Boyer, E. *High School: A Report on Secondary Education in America.* New York: Harper & Row, 1983.

Christ-Janer, A. "Institutional Mission in an Era of Retrenchment." *Liberal Education,* 66 (1980), pp. 161-168.

Cope, R.A. "Strategic Planning, Management, and Decision-Making." *AAHE/ERIC Higher Education Research Report No. 9.* Washington, D.C.: American Association for Higher Education, 1981.

Enthoven, A.C. "Measures of the Outputs of Higher Education: Some Practical Suggestions for Their Development and Use." In *Outputs of Higher Education.* Washington, D.C.: WICHE-ACE/CRDHE, July 1970, pp. 51-58.

Feistritzer, C. *The Condition of Teaching: A State by State Analysis.* Princeton, N.J.: The Carnegie Foundation for the Advancement of Teaching, 1983.

Feldman, K.A., and T.A. Newcomb. *The Impact of College on Students.* San Francisco: Jossey-Bass, 1969.

Finn, C. "Trying Higher Education: An Eight Count Indictment." *Change,* 16, No.4 (May/June 1984), pp. 28-32.

Flexner, A. *The American College: A Criticism.* New York: The Century Co., 1908 (rpt. New York: Arno Press and the New York Times, 1969).

Forrest, A. *Increasing Student Competence and Persistence: The Best Case for General Education.* Iowa City, IA: American College Testing, 1982.

Haskins, C. *The Rise of the Universities.* Ithaca, NY: Cornell University Press, 1957, p. 47.

Hutchins, R.M. "Interview with Robert Maynard Hutchins." *Chronicle of Higher Education* (May 23, 1977).

Jefferson, T. *A Bill for the More General Diffusion of Knowledge.* 1779, rpt. In *Crusade Against Ignorance.* Ed. G. Lee. New York: Teacher's College, Columbia University, 1969.

Justiz, M. quoted in *NIE Bulletin.* Washington, D.C.: National Institute on Education, Sept. 22, 1983.

Keeton, M. "An Approach to a Theory of Quality Control." In *Report on a Conference on Quality Control in Nontraditional Higher Education.* Columbia, MD: Antioch College, 1974.

Kiehle, F. "The Use of State Level Goals as the Basis for Assessing Postsecondary Education Performance." *Governor's Committee on Postsecondary Education,* October, 1981 (ERIC ED 211 024).

Lawrence, J.K., and K.C. Green. "A Question of Quality: The Higher Education Ratings Game." *AAHE-ERIC/Higher Education Research Report No.5.* Washington, D.C.: AAHE-ERIC, 1980.

Marcus, L., A. Leone, and E. Goldberg. "The Path to Excellence: Quality Assurance in Higher Education." Washington, D.C.: AAHE-ERIC, 1983.

Messick, S., and A. Jungeblut. "Time and Method in Coaching for the SAT." *Psychological Bulletin,* 89 (1981), pp. 191-216.

Morrison, S.E., *The Development of Harvard University Since the Inauguration of President Eliot 1869-1929.* Cambridge: Cambridge University Press, 1930, quoted in O'Neill, p. 72.

Naisbitt, J. *Megatrends: Ten New Directions Transforming Our Lives.* New York: Warner, 1982.

National Commission on Excellence in Education. "A Nation at Risk: The Imperative for Educational Reform." Washington, D.C.: U.S. Department of Education, 1983.

O'Neill, J. "Examinations and Quality Control" In *Meeting the New Demand for Standards.* Ed. J.R. Warren. San Francisco: Jossey-Bass, 1983, pp. 69-80.

Owens, W.A. "Background Data." In *Handbook of Industrial and Organizational Psychology.* Providence, RI: Brown, 1970.

Perlman, P. "New Tools and Techniques in University Administration." *Educational Record,* 55 (1979), pp. 34-42.

Peters, T., and R. Waterman. *In Search of Excellence: Lessons from America's Best-Run Companies.* New York: Harper & Row, 1982.

Prillaman, Major General J.A. quoted in Tice, J. "ROTC Cadets to be Tested on Basic Academic Skills." *Army Times,* March 22, 1984, p. 2.

Scott, R.A. "Program Review's Missing Member: A Consideration of Quality and Its Assessment," 1980 (ERIC ED 167 015).

Stevens, J., and B. Hamlett. "State Concerns for Learning: Quality and State Policy." In *Meeting the New Demand for Standards.* Ed. J.R. Warren. San Francisco: Jossey-Bass, 1983, pp. 29-38.

Struening, E., and M. Guttentag, eds. *Handbook of Evaluation Research.* Beverly Hills, CA: Sage, 1975.

U.S. Department of Education. *The Nation Responds: Recent Efforts to Improve Education.* Washington, D.C.: U.S. Government Printing Office, 1984.

APPENDICES

APPENDIX A

The Assessment Instruments

...elp determine the degree of success the University is having in achieving its goals and to focus institutional efforts, following types of instruments are used:

Standardized National Exams: NMSU feels that comparison of its students and their academic progress with other students throughout the nation by means of objective data is of considerable importance. Furthermore, it is vital to the institution that NMSU know the relative impact it is having on the student through value-added information.

    a. **Freshman Exam** to assess the general academic preparation that beginning students had in mathematics, social science, science, and English –

The American College Testing (ACT) Freshman College Entrance Exam is strongly recommended for all freshmen entering NMSU. Should freshmen enter NMSU without having taken this ACT exam, they are given the opportunity to take the test on campus without charge during a testing period early in the first semester of their matriculation.

    b. **Sophomore Exams** to measure general knowledge –

The ACT College Outcome Measures Project (COMP) exam and the ACT Residual Exam are used to measure the value added by the general education component of the curriculum. This assessment in value added began in 1975 with the testing of 952 entering freshmen utilizing the Sequential Test of Educational Progress (STEP). The STEP test was utilized to test freshmen in 1975 and 1976 and to reassess sophomores, who had taken STEP as freshmen, in 1977 and 1978. In 1978, the University began utilizing the ACT to measure growth in the basic skill areas. In the spring of 1981, the University initiated the use of the COMP/ACT exam to measure the value added. It had been recognized that both the ACT and STEP tests were too limiting in their scope. The ACT test was still administered to half of the sophomores in order to maintain baseline data.

    c. **Senior Exams** to measure specific knowledge and assess the performance of senior students on nationally established exams in their major area of study –

The program of testing was initiated in 1974, and now consists of the following examinations for students in the various disciplines.

The NTE, UAP, and GRE tests referred to above are developed by the Educational Testing Service of Princeton, N.J. have national college senior and graduate student norms.

Some of the tests administered to seniors in certain major fields will be the same tests administered as the "Gradua Record Examination" (GRE) advanced field tests used for admission to graduate schools. Students who take the GRE tests may specify that their scores be placed in the GRE history file for later reporting to graduate schools, professio schools, or scholarship sponsors.

The UAP, GRE, and NTE testing programs of ETS do not have major field examinations for all of the major fields offered at NMSU. In most instances, we have substituted a test which measures general cognitive ability, or the ability reason and solve problems in one's major field and in other life situations. This test is the College Outcome Measure Project (COMP) of the American College Testing Program. The COMP exam measures students' ability in six areas: communicating, solving problems, clarifying values, functioning within social institutions, using science and technolog and using the arts. Scores on this test have a rather substantial correlation with GPA's earned in one's major field a with cumulative GPA. Thus, we are able to approximate the level of performance a student would have on a comprehensive examination in a particular major field. In a few remaining instances, we have used locally developed tes

2. **Institutional Surveys:** To measure the quality of Northeast's students assumes the need for the collection c attitudinal data. Performance evaluation includes a subjective as well as an objective component. Therefore, NMSU conducts research to detemine how its students feel about their total experience at the University.

    a. **Survey of Students:** The University places high value on student response data to evaluate NMSU's contribution to their academic progress and personal experiences.

        1) The **Summer Orientation Student Questionnaire;** developed by NMSU and distributed to incoming freshman students.

        2) The **Institutional Student Survey (ISS);** developed by NMSU and distributed biennially to currently enrolled students.

        3) The **Graduating Student Questionnaire (GSQ);** developed by the National Center for Higher Education Management Systems and adapted for local use.

    b. **Survey of Alumni:** The University values the response of its graduates in assessing the effetiveness of its programs and services. A survey which includes both general (total university) and specific (individual program) questions is distributed to alumni triennially.

    c. **Survey of Employers:** The University recognizes the necessity to monitor the effectiveness its programs and the competency of its graduates through evaluations by employers. A firstyear teacher education survey is distributed annually; an additional survey of employers is c ducted triennially.

Divisions and Degrees	Required Senior Tests
BUSINESS DIVISION	
Accounting (BS)	AICPA-CATP Test
Bus. Admin. (BS)	UAP Business Test
Bus. Educ. (BS)	NTE (Bus. Ed. Test)
EDUCATION	
Elem. & Kind. Ed. (BSE)	NTE (Elem. Ed. Test)
FINE ARTS	
Art (Fine & Liberal) - (BA)	COMP Exam
Fine Arts (BA)	COMP Exam
Art Educ. (BSE)	NTE (Art Educ. Test)
Music Educ. (BME)	NTE (Mus. Ed. Test)
Music (BM)	NTE (Mus. Ed. Test)
Music (BA)	COMP Exam
Performing Arts (BA)	COMP Exam
HEALTH & P.E.	
Phys. Educ. (BSE)	NTE (Phys. Educ. Test)
Health; Recreat.; P.E. (BS)	UAP (Phys. Educ. Test)
HOME ECONOMICS	
Child Development (BS)	Local H.E. Comprehensive
Clothing, Text., Ret. (BS)	Local H.E. Comprehensive
General Home Econ. (BS)	Local H.E. Comprehensive
Voc. Home Econ. (BSE)	NTE (Home Econ. Ed. Test)
LANGUAGE & LITERATURE	
English (BA)	NTE (English, L & L Test)
English (BSE)	NTE (English, L & L Test)
French (BA) (BSE)	MLA COOP Test
Mass Communication (BA-BSE)	Cooperative English Test
Spanish (BS) (BSE)	MLA COOP Test
Communication Arts (BA)	NTE (Speech, Comm. & Theat)
Communication Arts (BSE)	NTE (Speech, Comm. & Theat)
Theatre (BA) (BSE)	NTE (Speech, Comm. & Theat)
Interpersonal Comm. (BA)	Local Comprehensive Exam
MATHEMATICS	
Mathematics (BS)	GRE (Mathematics Test)
Mathematics (BSE)	NTE (Math. Educ. Test)
Math. - Computer Science,(BS)	COMP Exam
NURSING	
Nursing (BSN)	National Council Licensure Exam

Division and Degrees	Required Senior Tests
PRACTICAL ARTS	
Agriculture Educ. (BSE)	Local Agriculture Exam
Agronomy (BS)	Local Agriculture Exam
Animal Science (BS)	Local Agriculture Exam
Driver & Safety Educ. (BSE)	COMP Exam
General Agriculture (BS)	Local Agriculture Exam
Industrial Educ. (BSE)	NTE (Ind. Arts Educ. Test)
Industrial Occup. (BS)	Local Ind. Occup. Exam
Industrial Tech. (BS)	Local Ind. Tech. Exam
SCIENCE	
Biology (BS)	UAP (Biology Test)
Biology (BSE)	NTE (Biol. & Gen. Sci.)
Botany (BS)	UAP (Biology Test)
Chemistry (BS) (BSE)	GRE (Chemistry Test)
Environ. Sci. (BS) (BSE)	COMP Exam
Comprehensive Sci. (BSE)	NTE (Biol. & Gen. Sci.)
Earth Science (BSE)	NTE (Biol. & Gen. Sci.)
Physics (BS) (BSE)	GRE (Physics Test)
Zoology (BS)	UAP (Biology Test)
Med. Technology (BS)	UAP (Biology Test)
SOCIAL SCIENCE	
Economics (BA-BS)	GRE (Economics Test)
Economics (BSE)	NTE (Soc. Studies Test)
Geography (BA-BS)	GRE (Geography Test)
Geography (BSE)	NTE (Soc. Studies Test)
History (BA-BS)	GRE (History Test)
History (BSE)	NTE (Soc. Studies Test)
Law Enforcement (BS)	Local Crim. Justice Exam
Phil. & Religion (BA)	GRE (Philosophy)
Polit. Sci. (BA-BS)	GRE (Political Sci. Test)
Polit. Sci. (BSE)	NTE (Soc. Studies Test)
Psychology (BA-BS-BSE)	GRE (Psychology Test)
Social Science (BSE)	NTE (Soc. Studies Test)
Sociology (BA-BS)	GRE (Sociology Test)
Sociology (BSE)	NTE (Soc. Studies Test)
SPECIAL PROGRAMS	
Special Education (BSE)	NTE (Elem. Educ. Test)
Speech Path. (BA-BS-BSE)	COMP Exam

APPENDIX B

Articles published in student newspaper:

Northeast Missouri State University

index

Kirksville, Mo. 63501

4 INDEX Thursday, Nov. 10, 1983

EDITORIAL

Seniors urged to take test seriously

Senior tests will be held Nov. 8 through Dec. 10 for all seniors graduating in December or graduating in May and not attending NMSU during the spring semester.

These tests are designed to measure a student's competency in his area of study, to determine how well a student ranks against other students across the country and to evaluate this institution's programs, Darrell Krueger, dean of instruction, said.

Right now the tests are not graduation requirements in the capacity that students must score at a certain percentile before they can graduate but only that the tests have to be taken before graduation is approved.

For this reason, some seniors look at the tests as only a formality to graduation and do not realize their importance. The tests do have an effect on the University.

For example, in fiscal year 1981 NMSU received $00,000 from the Coordinating Board for Higher Education on the promise that the institution would show certain improvements, including test scores. Since that time, NMSU has submitted yearly reports to the budget officer of the board's administration for review of test scores.

This year the board has recommended that NMSU receive another $500,000 with provisions that the University again show gains in test scores as part of the value-added program.

While the University has been able to meet the provisions set by the board and continue receiving funding for improvements, there is always the possibility that this financial source could fall through if test scores do not reflect the institution's promise of improvement. By not taking a serious attitude toward the tests, students could be hurting the strong case for funding requests which the University has been able to employ so far.

The University encourages academic advisers to talk with students about the importance of senior tests. Some divisions have senior seminars and other division heads go into senior-level classes to discuss the tests.

Even with this encouragement, the final decision is left up to the students about whether the senior tests really matter. Although the scores do not become a part of the transcript or determine the approval for graduation, they do count for something. The future ability of this institution to continue to implement quality education rests upon the receipt of necessary funding from the state.

Value-added hearings clarify concept's role, justify effectiveness

by Verna Elrod

This is part one of a series on the Student Senate value – added hearings.

Student Senate value – added hearings began Tuesday and will continue every Tuesday and Wednesday through Feb. 8 with a final session set for Feb. 15. They are being held in the Alumni Room of the Student Union Building.

The hearings last two hours, from 6:30-8:30 p.m. on Tuesdays and from 4-6 p.m. on Wednesdays. They are designed to clarify what value added is doing, said Chuck Woods, co-chairman of the senate's value – added hearing committee.

Each night different faculty and administrative personnel will speak and answer questions. Six divisions, social science, mathematics, science, language and literature, business and education will be represented.

The hearings are open to everyone, but because of the time element, the only students asking questions will be those on a special 8-member panel. The student panel changes every night depending on who is scheduled to speak.

Woods said, "We're hoping to help show what the six divisions have done and where they need to improve."

"We're trying to help ourselves get a better education," said Sharon Weiner, co-chairman of the value – added hearing committee.

During Tuesday night's hearing, Robert Dager, head of the Division of Business, said some students complain that value added is making them work too hard. "They don't understand it's (value added) learning," he said.

Jack Magruder, professor of science, said that value added is not perfect, but negative attitudes are a result of being misinformed.

"The whole program is not set in concrete. There is room for making changes. I would never view value added as 'we have arrived,'" Magruder said.

Woods said value added is a way for the University to rate itself and that students should fight for it so they can be sure they are getting a quality education.

Dager said inflating grading scales and assigning "busy work" are not part of value added. But he said it could mean more homework because the classes are teaching more in the same amount of time.

Dager said nothing was being done in his division about inflated grading scales. "If it became a problem, I would discuss it with the faculty," he said.

Value added is learning, Dager said. The results of the sophomore and senior tests are used to revise the curriculum. It lets the University know what areas need work.

"We used test results to set goals and for budget requests from the state legislature," Dager said. The Division of Business received extra money and used it for faculty development, he said.

Weiner said the first night of hearings went well. "It went a little long, but it's so difficult to keep it short."

The senate will publish a report on the hearings for the students along with recommendations on how value added can be improved. Woods said this report would be available sometime after spring break.

At Wednesday's hearing, Terry Smith, dean of students; Tom Shrout, director of external relations; Vonnie Nichols, director of student activities; and Mike Kacir, director of testing services, answered questions. Their comments will be reported in next week's Index.

On Jan. 24, Daniel Ball, head of the Division of Education; Dale Schatz, University vice-president; Jack Magruder, professor of science, and Candy Young, assistant professor of political science, are scheduled to speak.

Faculty from the Division of Business will speak on Jan. 25. The faculty from the Division of Education will speak on Jan.31; and faculty from the divisions of Language and Literature, Mathematics and Science will speak on Feb. 1,7 and 8 respectively. Darrell Krueger, dean of instruction, will speak on Feb. 15.

FROM THE STAFF
Value added overlooked; pressure is own creation

The University is proud of its value-added concept, and deservedly, but of all the various aspects of the program there is one addition which is rarely mentioned.

The program adds value to the coursework we do. It adds to the value of the education we receive. It also adds to the pressure of obtaining a college education.

Pressure is part of the college experience. I expect it, and I can cope with it, usually. I use pressure to motivate myself, but there are limits. Unfortunately, too often, I and many others do not recognize those limits, or we ignore them.

Value added was established to measure the progress made throughout the college experience, and I believe it has added a great deal of quality to my education. With each step I have made toward successful completion of my degree, it has also added to the pressure.

The pressure is not necessarily bad, either.

The pressure I am feeling in class is usually because the class is challenging. That has not always been true in the past. I would rather take challenging classes. Challenging classes have something to offer; they make me learn.

If I am to be honest, I must admit that a lot of the pressure I feel is not forced upon me by value added but is of my own creation.

I do not believe I can get the most out of college by going to classes, studying and going home. I am a firm believer in the value of involvement and practical experience. Sometimes it gets me in trouble.

Because I like to get involved in activities outside of class, I tend to go to extremes. Whoever advised moderation in all things should have shouted at me a little louder.

I have watched friends get involved beyond their ability to complete their obligations, and I always swore I would never do that. I was wrong. I am beginning to think it is a senior syndrome. It has caused me to make some difficult decisions lately. Decisions I would have given anything to avoid. But I could not.

Pressure can be a valuable ally when trying to meet a deadline. Deadlines don't upset me. I understand their importance, and I meet them. I have to.

Pressure can also be a deadly enemy. When you have overextended yourself, every second of every day seems to be overrun with obligations which must be met, meetings to attend, telephone calls to make, people to find and work to do.

When I commit to an organization or activity, I try to devote as much time as it needs in order to make operations run smoothly. I place pressure upon myself.

I volunteer when I should fade into the background. I choose to be involved rather than just there. If the only reason I attend is to warm a chair, I have made a mistake. I am not contributing and should not be there.

I believe in the principle. The problem is adjusting my involvement to include only those things which are most important, which allow me time to do them properly and which allow me time to do well in my classes.

Pressure returns. A poor decision throws off the entire schedule. A miscalculation in determining a time commitment causes chaos.

The greater the pressure, the more successfully I complete my tasks—up to a point. Then the effects of the pressure begin to outweigh the motivation it offers.

Too much pressure makes me miserable. My friends begin to avoid me. I am not a pleasant person to be around. My classwork suffers; I tend to forget classes have outside work when I am distracted by outside obligations.

It is a confusion many people face, and it is not that difficult to avoid. But, small problems seem magnified when, as a senior, I realize I also have to pinpoint career goals, I have to fill out all the paperwork involved in graduation, I have to find a job and complete a thousand other little details before I leave.

Fulfilling obligations now seems very important to my future.

Fulfilling obligations is important, but getting priorities straight is probably more important. I have enjoyed most of my involvement, but I could have managed it much better.

I have added value to my education through my involvement. My education would not have been complete without it. It would have been easier without all of the pressure, but it would not have been better.

Kathleen Armentrout is a senior mass communication major from Salisbury, Mo. She is copy editor for the Index.

APPENDIX C

NORTHEAST MISSOURI STATE UNIVERSITY
GRADUATING STUDENT QUESTIONNAIRE

Dear Graduating Student of Northeast,

    Congratulations to you on the educational achievement for which you will soon be formally recognized! We hope that Northeast Missouri State University has made a positive difference in your intellectual, career, and personal life. It goes without saying that our graduates have made a positive difference to Northeast in the past and undoubtedly will do so, perhaps even more so, in the future. We wish you every success!

    As you complete this portion of your education, we ask for your honest responses on this questionnaire. In its efforts to evaluate its effectiveness in promoting constructive student growth, the University counts on your input. Please give us your serious attention in responding to this questionnaire.

    Thank you! And the best to you in the future!

                                Sincerely,

                                  Charles J. McClain
                                  President

INSTRUCTIONS: *Specific directions are given for completing many of the questions in this survey. If no directions are given, please check the number of the most appropriate response. Kindly ignore the figures in parentheses; they are for computer coding purposes.*

(1-9) Student Identification Number: ___ ___ ___ -- ___ ___ -- ___ ___ ___

(10) What is your sex?
    1 ___ Male
    2 ___ Female

(11) Are you currently married?
    1 ___ Yes
    2 ___ No

(12) How old are you?
    1 ___ 20 or under
    2 ___ 21 or 22
    3 ___ 23 or 24
    4 ___ 25 or 26
    5 ___ 27 to 29
    6 ___ 30 to 39
    7 ___ 40 to 61
    8 ___ 62 or over

(13) Where is your permanent home located?
1 ___ Kirksville
2 ___ Other Northeast Missouri
3 ___ St. Louis area
4 ___ Other area in Missouri
5 ___ Iowa
6 ___ Illinois
7 ___ Other state or country

(14) How would you describe yourself? Mark only one.
1 ___ Afro-American/Black
2 ___ American Indian or Alaskan Native
3 ___ Caucasian American/White
4 ___ Mexican American/Chicano
5 ___ Asian American, Oriental, or Pacific Islander
6 ___ Puerto Rican, Cuban, or other Hispanic Origin
7 ___ Other
8 ___ Prefer not to respond

(15) What has been your residence classification at NMSU?
1 ___ In-state student
2 ___ Out-of-state student
3 ___ International student (not a U. S. citizen)

(16) Where did you rank in your high school class based on grades earned?
1 ___ Lowest quartile (0 to 24%-ile)
2 ___ Second quartile (25 to 49%-ile)
3 ___ Third quartile (50 to 74%-ile)
4 ___ Top quartile (75 to 99%-ile)

(17) What type of school did you attend just prior to entering NMSU?
1 ___ Public High School
2 ___ Private High School
3 ___ Vocational/Technical School
4 ___ Two-year College
5 ___ Four-year College/University
6 ___ Other (Specify) _____

(18) How many years have you attended this university for the current degree? (Check to the nearest year.)
1 ___ 1 year
2 ___ 2 years
3 ___ 3 years
4 ___ 4 years
5 ___ 5 or more years

(19) What was your enrollment status while attending this university?
1 ___ Primarily full-time (12 semester hours or more)
2 ___ Primarily part-time (less than 12 semester hours)

(20) Did you transfer credits from another college or university to NMSU toward your degree?
1 ___ Yes
2 ___ No

(21-23) Indicate your major at this university. Please use the list of college majors and occupation choices included with this survey (gray sheet); select the three-digit code, and write the code in the boxes below. If undecided, mark "Undecided--000."

(24-26) What degree are you currently receiving from this university, and what is the highest degree you plan to ultimately earn? Please check a number in each column.

CURRENT ULTIMATE
1 ___   1 ___   Not seeking a certificate nor a degree
2 ___   2 ___   Certificate
3 ___   3 ___   BSE/BME degree
4 ___   4 ___   BA/BM degree
5 ___   5 ___   BS/BSN degree
6 ___   6 ___   MA teaching degree
7 ___   7 ___   MS/MA non-teaching degree
8 ___   8 ___   Education Specialist
         9 ___   Professional degree
        10 ___   Doctoral degree (e.g., Ph. D., Ed. D.)

(27) Are you currently working at or have you secured a full-time job (35 hours or more a week) in which you plan to work once you graduate. Please check only one.
1 ___ Yes, I will continue working in the job I had before graduating
2 ___ Yes, I just recently obtained a new job
3 ___ Yes, I am a homemaker, not employed outside the home
4 ___ No, but I am looking for a job
5 ___ No, but I intend to look for a job in the next six months
6 ___ No, and I do not intend to look for a job in the next six months

(28) Indicate your rating of NMSU at the time you applied for admission.
1 ____ It was my first choice
2 ____ It was my second choice
3 ____ It was my third choice
4 ____ It was my fourth choice or lower

(29) If you could start college over, would you choose to attend this university?
1 ____ Definitely Yes
2 ____ Probably Yes
3 ____ Uncertain
4 ____ Probably No
5 ____ Definitely No

(30) If you could start college over, would you choose the same major?
1 ____ Definitely Yes
2 ____ Probably Yes
3 ____ Uncertain
4 ____ Probably No
5 ____ Definitely No

(31) How would you compare the quality of education provided at this university with that of other universities/colleges?
1 ____ Unable to judge
2 ____ Worse
3 ____ About the same
4 ____ Better

(32) Besides the financial benefits, has your college education thus far improved the quality of your life?
1 ____ Definitely Yes
2 ____ Probably Yes
3 ____ Uncertain
4 ____ Probably No
5 ____ Definitely No

(33-34) What was your single most important reason for attending NMSU? Check only one.

PRIMARY REASON
1 ____ Cost
2 ____ Admissions Standards
3 ____ Social Atmosphere
4 ____ Location
5 ____ Type of Programs Available
6 ____ Academic Reputation
7 ____ Availability of Scholarship/Financial Aid
8 ____ Advise of Parents or Relatives
9 ____ Advice of High School Personnel
10 ____ To be with Friends
11 ____ Other (Specify)

(35-36) What was your second most important reason for attending NMSU? Check one.

SECONDARY REASON
1 ____ Cost
2 ____ Admissions Standards
3 ____ Social Atmosphere
4 ____ Location
5 ____ Type of Programs Available
6 ____ Academic Reputation
7 ____ Availability of Scholarship/Financial Aid
8 ____ Advise of Parents or Relatives
9 ____ Advice of High School Personnel
10 ____ To be with Friends
11 ____ Other (Specify)

What is your impression of NMSU at the present time? Please check your feelings about the various aspects listed. The higher the number you choose, the more you agree with the statement on the right; the lower the number you choose, the more you agree with the statement on the left. Leave blank any item about which you do not know.

Example: low quality food service | 1 | 2 | 3 | 4 X | high quality food service

If you felt the food was of very high quality, you would check 4.

---

		low 1 2	high 3 4	
(37)	low quality programs			high quality programs
(38)	unfriendly school			friendly school
(39)	no selection in admission			selective admission
(40)	high cost			low cost
(41)	poor social life			good social life
(42)	poor residence halls			good residence halls
(43)	inaccessible			easy to attend (accessible)
(44)	limited programs			diverse programs
(45)	poor faculty			good faculty
(46)	poor library			good library
(47)	poor facilities			good facilities
(48)	large school			small school
(49)	liberal			conservative
(50)	urban school			rural school
(51)	low quality athletics			high quality athletics

GSQ, Page 4

Starting with the freshman year in college, how many semester hours of the following subjects have you successfully completed?

```
                                    0 = none
                                    1 = three semester hours
                                    2 = six semester hours
                                    3 = nine semester hours
                                    4 = twelve semester hours or more
```

(52) English
(53) Mathematics
(54) Science
(55) Foreign Language
(56) Computer Science
(57) Social Science
(58) Fine Arts

(59) Approximately how many hours per week did you spend on college homework?
1 ___ 0 - 5 hours   3 ___ 11 - 15 hours   5 ___ 21 - 25 hours
2 ___ 6 - 10 hours   4 ___ 16 - 20 hours   6 ___ 26 or more hours

(60) How often were term papers, reports or major writing assignments required in your courses? Please mark only one.
1 ___ Never
2 ___ Not very often
3 ___ Often
4 ___ Very often

(61) How often did you regularly use a textbook? Please check only on response.
1 ___ In none of my classes
2 ___ In a few of my classes
3 ___ In most of my classes
4 ___ In all of my classes

Please indicate to the best of your ability the number of times you involved yourself in the following activities during the course of the school year.

```
        Once a week or more
        About once a month
        About once every two months
        Once or twice during the year
        Never
        1  2  3  4  5
```

(62) Discussed serious topics with students whose opinions and personal values differed from your own
(63) Looked at situations/issues and attempted to develop a solution
(64) Asked for the criticism of others on your writings or speaking
(65) Used library resources to gather research materials and information
(66) Initiated an appointment with a faculty member or administrator to gain needed information
(67) Outlined/highlighted major concepts of readings, class notes, and study materials
(68) Revised/rewrote essays, term papers, and other assignments to improve your style and techniques of writing
(69) Attended a cultural activity sponsored or performed by the university or a student group

The following statements reflect goals of many college students. How much help do you feel the experiences at this university gave you in reaching these goals?

```
        This university gave very much help
        This university gave some help
        This university gave very little help
        This university gave no help
        This was not a goal of mine
        0  1  2  3  4
```

(70) To increase my knowledge in my academic field
(71) To satisfy job and career requirements
(72) To obtain a degree or certificate
(73) To learn skills that will enrich my daily life
(74) To become actively involved in student life and activities
(75) To develop greater appreciation of cultural events
(76) To improve my self-image
(77) To improve my leadership skills
(1) To increase my earning power
(2) To generally improve myself

[TURN TO PAGE 5]

How adequate do you feel your education at NMSU has been in each of the following?

Very adequate — 1
Somewhat adequate — 2
Somewhat inadequate — 3
Very inadequate — 4

General Education Skills

#	Item	1	2	3	4
(3)	Writing effectively				
(4)	Speaking effectively				
(5)	Understanding written information				
(6)	Working independently				
(7)	Managing personal/family finances				
(8)	Learning on your own				
(9)	Understanding graphic information				
(10)	Using the library				
(11)	Following directions				
(12)	Understanding consumer issues				
(13)	Caring for your own physical and mental health				
(14)	Working cooperatively in a group				
(15)	Organizing your time effectively				
(16)	Recognizing your rights, responsibilities, and privileges as a citizen				
(17)	Planning and carrying out projects				
(18)	Understanding and applying mathematics				
(19)	Understanding different philosophies and cultures				
(20)	Persisting at difficult tasks				
(21)	Defining and solving problems				
(22)	Understanding the interaction of man and the environment				
(23)	Leading/guiding others				
(24)	Recognizing assumptions, making logical inferences, and reaching correct conclusions				
(25)	Understanding and appreciating the arts				
(26)	Understanding and applying scientific principles and methods				

How adequately has the program of your major prepared you in the following? If you feel an item does not apply, please mark "0."

Very adequately — 1
Somewhat adequately — 2
Somewhat inadequately — 3
Very inadequately — 4
Does not apply — 0

Knowledge — KNOWLEDGE OF --

#	Item	0	1	2	3	4
(27)	Subject matter and processes of your specialty (major)					
(28)	Issues and trends pertinent to your specialty					
(29)	Concepts of human growth/development pertinent to your specialty					
(30)	Theories pertinent to your specialty					
(31)	Alternative strategies for applying skills of your specialty					
(32)	Management and organizational skills of your specialty					

Abilities — ABILITY TO --

#	Item	0	1	2	3	4
(33)	Apply knowledge in defining problems and solving them					
(34)	Establish a productive environment on and off the job					
(35)	Respond to people from different social and cultural backgrounds on formal and informal occasions					
(36)	Formulate plans and make appropriate applications					
(37)	Select and use appropriate materials/aids					
(38)	Evaluate success of performance in career					
(39)	Communicate ideas clearly and simply in correct English					
(40)	Find information; interpret and apply findings					
(41)	Identify values and respond ethically					
(42)	Integrate career and personal goals					
(43)	Meet responsibilities of citizenship					

Attitudes — ATTITUDE OF --

#	Item	0	1	2	3	4
(44)	Believing that learning is a life-long process					
(45)	Respecting the uniqueness and worth of each individual					
(46)	Accepting responsibility of preparing for the future					
(47)	Confidence in your personal competence					

GSQ, Page 6

Using the descriptors below, how would you rate yourself on a scale of 1 (low) to 4 (high)?

	low	high				low	high
	1 2 3 4					1 2 3 4	
(48)		Independent, self-reliant		(55)			Competent culturally
(49)		Adaptable, able to adjust to people and situations		(56)			Understanding of own abilities, interests, and personality
(50)		Skilled in solving problems		(57)			Able to manage emotions
(51)		Skilled in communicating					Able to identify values and
(52)		Competent intellectually		(58)			respond ethically
(53)		Competent physically		(59)			Prepared for world of work
(54)		Competent socially		(60)			Literate as a citizen

How satisfied were you with the experiences, services and facilities at NMSU as listed below? Please check one answer for each statement.

Very satisfied ------------------------------
Somewhat satisfied ----------------------
Somewhat dissatisfied -----------------
Very dissatisfied -----------------
Does not apply ---------------

			0 1 2 3 4
(61)		Your overall impression of general education courses	
(62)		Your overall impression of courses in your major	
(63)	*Instructional*	The overall quality of instruction in your major	
(64)		The availability of courses offered in your major	
(65)		The accessibility of instructors in your major	
(66)		The helpfulness of instructors in assisting with career plans	
(67)		Faculty academic advising	
(68)		The attitude of faculty toward students	
(69)		The attitude of non-teaching staff toward students	
(70)		Admissions Office	
(71)		Registrar's Office	
(72)	*Offices*	Financial Aid Office	
(73)		Career/Placement Office	
(74)		Student Activities Office	
(75)		Freshman Counseling	
(76)		Testing Services	
(77)		Career Planning Services	
(1)		Placement Services	
(2)		Food Services	
(3)		Student Health Services	
(4)		Library Services	
(5)		Campus Bookstore Services	
(6)	*Services*	Safety and Security Services	
(7)		Recreational and Intramural Programs and Services	
(8)		Reading and Writing Skills Improvement Services	
(9)		Math Skills Improvement Services	
(10)		Academic Computer Services	
(11)		Student Government	
(12)		Personal Counseling	
(13)		New-Student Orientation Program	
(14)		Residence Life Services	
(15)		Campus Media (student newspaper, yearbook, etc.)	
(16)		Registration Procedures	
(17)		Library Facilities	
(18)		Study Areas	
(19)	*Facilities*	Computer Facilities	
(20)		Housing Facilities	
(21)		Athletic Facilities	
(22)		Parking Facilities	
(23)		Laboratory/instructional Equipment	
(24)		Concern for you as an individual	
(25)	*General*	Racial harmony at this university	
(26)		General condition the buildings and grounds at this university	
(27)		This university in general	

(28) How well do you feel NMSU has prepared you for continuing education?
1 ___ Do not plan to continue education   4 ___ Somewhat adequately
2 ___ Poorly   5 ___ Very adequately
3 ___ Somewhat inadequately

LD
4008
.I5
1984

In pursuit of degrees with
  integrity : a value added
  approach to undergraduate
  assessment